A Donauschwabian Diary

Displaced But Not Forgotten

Magdalena Wetzer

Copyright © 2017 by Magdalena Wetzer

All rights reserved. This book or any portion thereof may not be reproduced or used in any manner whatsoever without the express written permission of the publisher except for the use of brief quotations in a book review or scholarly journal.

First Edition
ISBN 978-0-9994235-0-9
Published by Nicholas Dean Pentcheff

This book is set in Futura ND (Bauer Types, S.L.). Body text is Book 11/14 and headings are Medium 16.5/21. Futura, designed by Paul Renner, was released in Germany in 1927. The release of Futura ND by Neufville Digital restored the small capitals (used in the running heads) and old-style figures of Renner's original.

Contents

Foreword v
Preface ix
1. Hostile Intentions at the Border 1
2. Walk to Freedom 9
3. Shocking News From Across the Border. 13
4. In Johannisfeld, 1946 25
5. Austria In Sight 31
6. Nani and Josep Travel to Vienna 37
7. Nineteen and On My Own 43
8. Next Stop, Austria 45
9. Stammersdorf, Austria 49
10. We Settle in Vienna 59
11. Our New Address 63
12. Making New Friends 65
13. Trouble at Work 69
14. My Lucky Monday 75
15. Going My Own Way 83
16. Dating at Twenty-One 85
17. Big Changes Ahead 89
18. Vacation Time 91
19. Surprises 95
20. November 99
21. Awaiting Spring 107
22. Warmer Weather 111
23. Spirit of the Danube 115
24. Where To Next? 121

Foreword

When we learned that Mom was going to school to learn how to write the "story of her life" at the Torrance Adult School, we had no idea that the "project" itself would come to actually change her life over the twenty years she has been attending. (Humorous side note: some of Mom's European relatives, having heard of the length of time she has been attending, question why she keeps failing and ask if she will ever graduate...). We had heard the fragments of stories along with anecdotes and vignettes of her amazing life experience. The enormity of capturing it all into prose to preserve for our families and future generations seemed daunting to say the least.

Guided by the wisdom and endless patience of her teacher, Ruth Herbert, Mom began writing short stories to present to the class as a part of every Friday's assignment. We never witnessed the actual class sessions so we cannot comment on the exact process of how the class actually works. We do surmise, however, that listening to similar stories of harrowing experiences, hearing Ruth's compassionate but firm guidance, and experiencing the catharsis afforded by sympathetic ears, have improved Mom's writing and bestowed a greater sense of peace.

We cannot fathom the hardship, cruelty and hopelessness a war can exact upon individuals, families and entire communities. We weren't there. But as Mom continued to write, we began to understand the context of the stories she, Dad, and our Grandparents told. We are enormously grateful to our Grandmother, Anna, to have compelled Mom to start writing it down. As it turns out, Dad, who in the early years of Mom's going to class found the whole endeavor amusing, began attending as well. Soon he began to participate and write stories we recalled having heard repeatedly during our childhood. We are forever grateful to Ruth to have provided this framework and support.

On this, Mom's 90th birthday, we have stepped in to help turn her collected short stories into this book. Since Mom is not a native English speaker/writer, her mental translation from German has been challenging. Thus we have added to, or attempted to clarify, what Mom meant to say when she

PREFACE

wrote this or that passage. We would like to believe that we have made positive enhancements, but until Mom reads this, we are keeping our fingers crossed.

Gratefully,
Regina, Michael, Rudi, Dean, Christy, Jill, Katie, and fur children Sophie and Lilly

Preface

In 1997, my then 90 year old mother asked, "What can we give the children to remember us by?" My husband suggested I write our family history. At age 70 I went back to school to "Write the Story of My Life" in a Torrance, California adult class. Although English is not my native language, I quickly felt comfortable in the company of very friendly seniors, who like me, had the same goal. Sharing and exchanging stories with a great diversity of classmates from every corner of the world improved my English. I am enormously grateful to Ruth Herbert, our wonderful teacher, many inspiring classmates, and my patient and supportive family.

Wars of any kind inflict pain and suffering on countless innocent civilians. They cause wholesale physical destruction, the irreplaceable loss of a sense of security, harrowing tales of survival and struggle against all odds to regain a normal life. Sharing my stories with you is a means of speaking for millions of war victims. This has

A Donauschwabian Diary

been a very painful, yet rewarding experience and contributes to my healing process.

1. Hostile Intentions at the Border

Post WWII borders in Europe in 1946 were much in dispute between the former states of Yugoslavia, Romania and Hungary. They were patrolled, but by their detached understanding and ignorance of the ethnic and cultural heritage of the region, Roosevelt, Churchill, and Stalin crafted new borders whose boundaries put law and order in serious jeopardy. Survival teetered between fate and luck for millions of people displaced and separated from family and home.

My father, Josef Rosenzweig, served as a soldier in the Third Reich as a Yugoslavian citizen, and was conscripted to a military police unit. After May 8, 1945, at the official end of the war, his unit was dissolved in Lower-Austria. Without receiving discharge papers, every man was left to manage on his own. With no money or resources, his first challenge was to trade his uniform for civilian clothing. He found a local farmer willing to take him on as a field helper without pay. A farmer himself, and of a good-hearted nature, he set about to help this farmer improve some of this region's poor "Mühlviertel" farming practices. The local farmer's stubbornness prevailed, loudly declaring, "My father worked like this, and I am not going to change anything." Discouraged, Father chose to quickly move on.

Josef was in his mid forties and by sheer chance met up with a younger, twenty year old Sepp Achenbach, the son of close hometown friends from their village of Pardan. They had a shared predicament. No identification, no resources and a long distance from home. Sepp and Josef began the roughly 150 km walk home together, heading south towards Yugoslavia. A calming breeze and the gentle interplay of light and dark from the half moon encouraged their souls and they pushed on with no rest. They were hungry and thirsty. It was cold, but their brisk pace kept their bodies warm. On the barren path they continued towards a building with a dim light in a window. The two companions hoped to find friendly and inviting people in the former farmhouse.

Suddenly the peaceful silence of the night was shattered, when from behind a bush, only a stone's throw away, a com-

HOSTILE INTENTIONS AT THE BORDER

manding voice of a man shouted "STOJ" (Stop). The two travelers immediately froze and realized that they had arrived at the Yugoslav border. Their obedience brought them face to face with an armed border patrol guard. They responded promptly in the guards' Serbian language, and called back: "Please don't shoot. We are unarmed civilians — citizens from this region of the Banat."

"Shut up", shouted the guard. "With your hands up, keep marching toward the house with the light in the window!" A second, and then a third guard appeared, treating them like dangerous wild animals, chasing them toward the two room building.

As they entered, a kerosene lantern was shining into their shocked and tired faces. The warm temperature in the room came from a wood-burning stove on which some food was cooking. Near the table was a man dressed in an officer's uniform eating bread and drinking wine. He appeared to be the commanding chief of the local border patrol. He was unarmed, but had a mean looking expression in his face. His hostility was similar to that of the by now six other guards with menacing glares.

Now declared prisoners, Josef and Sepp were paraded in front of the commander and ordered to keep their hands up while being subjected to questioning. They were not asked for their names nor identification, only their destination. My father, being the older of the two, answered in the language the questions were posed, stating that they were unarmed farmers on their way to tend their livestock and to work their fields. The officer interrupted him yelling, "You show a bulge under your jacket!" and ordered the guards to search him for a weapon. All they found was a little wooden box tucked under his shirt close to his heart. It contained Josef's shaving kit and my picture as a 16 year old. It revealed nothing of military value and was thrown on the floor next to his feet.

The commander rose and stood in front of the prisoners and shouted into their ears, "While you were strolling through the landscape, believing in your innocence, many things have changed in this territory! Josip Bros Tito — our Communist president — has implemented new orders and rules, which proclaim that no property, land, or farm is yours anymore. It belongs to all of us, we the people who were born here with the language we speak. You are of a different kind, you no longer have a claim of citizenship, and you missed the deadline of reentry. Turn around and go back. But before you take another step, take off your boots and leave them here along with your jackets!"

"Please have mercy!" Josef pleaded. "Let us keep our pants and shirts and the wooden box!" This wish was granted him. Josef believed for the rest of his life, the Spirit of the little wooden box saved his life.

The guards, some not older than 13 to 14 years of age, and barely taller than the rifles they carried, were triumphant and jubilant as they watched the prisoners take their boots off, exposing their bare toes through the worn and dirty socks. They prized and sized the boots for themselves. Then the door opened and the two men were thrown out. Their bodies felt powerless and their minds disoriented. Numb, cold and confused, they barely heard the guard's next command yelled into the cold and the now awful and frightening night: "Now turn and run to the North, don't look back, don't look to the stars, just head straight out toward the city lights on the far horizon!" Terrified by this new reality and with only a small ray of hope for survival, they ran and dodged the hissing and flying rifle shots fired by the guards behind them. With the protection of night and Mother Nature's salvation they reached the city of Segedin in Hungary.

A Donauschwabian Diary

Josef and Sepp's goal was to find the prison in Segedin for a roof over their heads and food of any kind. They were quickly interned in the crowded facility, run by Russian officers, determined to mete out a harsh and repetitious routine on their prisoners. Days and weeks passed in the prison. One day my father approached an officer and politely suggested to him, speaking in Russian (he had learned Russian as a teenager from a prisoner of war during WWI). "Why not let a small group of harmless inmates, accompanied by guards, go to farmers in the region and work as field hands? The only payoff to them should be food eaten on location. This is a saving for the prison." The plan worked, and my father and others occasionally saw some daylight for a few days while helping the farmers tend their fields. Dada Cristifor, on old Serbian man, picked Josef because he was communicating in perfect Serbian and was a farmer himself. Since the prisoners were not to be paid money, and my father was so poor, he was unable to buy a postage stamp. The old, kind and respectful man gave him a postcard.

Not long thereafter a large commotion occurred in the prison with the arrival of new people. They were mainly young women who were released from Russia. They looked sick, suffering from malnutrition and were dressed in ragged clothing. Yugoslavia deprived them of the return to their homeland too, just like Josef and Sepp, on account of their German, Donauschwaben heritage. Instead, they were chased or shipped back to Hungary. Upon hearing this news, my father took my picture from the wooden box, showed it around asking, "Has anyone seen this girl?" One woman who was born in Stefansfeld came to him and stated the girl was from Pardan, a neighbor town in the Yugoslavian Banat. Very excited my father told her, "She is my daughter!" His next question, "Is she alive?"

"Yes," was her answer. My father thanked God for the good news and the woman for knowing by heart the address of the slave labor camp in Krivoj Rog, Russia — Sochorod No. 1 where I was being held.

He was hoping to make another attempt to go home after more political stability in Europe was established. Josef knew that he could now use his postcard to let me know he was alive. Having no stamp, he marked it in Hungarian words: "prisoner of war mail." Dada Christifor dropped the postcard in the mailbox. It arrived in Russia two months later. It renewed my hope to someday be reunited with my parents.

2. Walk to Freedom

My father's name was pronounced "Josep." My mother was known by her nickname "Nani," for Anna. It was 1946, during the greatest chaotic migration of refugees in Europe following WWII. Freedom was not served on a silver platter, but in painful and arduous footsteps. Whether trying to go home, finding a new one, or looking for relatives separated from each other in a fragmented Europe, people lived in an atmosphere best compared to quicksand. Nothing was stable, secure or reliable and everything seemed to try to pull you under and suffocate you. Transportation was by train or other rolling conveyance — no jet service. Walking, according to your own ability and contending with challenging circumstances along the way, was the most reliable way to reach a destination. Some travelers got lucky and skirted danger. Some were warned in time of pending danger. Others sadly became the victims whose only hope and prayer was to be rescued by passersby.

A Donauschwabian Diary

After Josep's first attempt to go home, getting caught at the Yugoslav border, then chased back to Hungary and imprisoned in Segedin for entering the country illegally, his second opportunity came when he was finally released from the prison. He headed back toward Lower-Austria where he was planning to go southeast via Romania and attempt entry to Yugoslavia at the central border into the Banat region. He met up with a large convoy of displaced people, mainly Donauschwaben farmers, who had been evacuated from the Romanian Banat in 1944 to escape the brutality of the occupying Russian Army. Germany had promised them and their families protection.

The Banat region was as flat as a tabletop. Horse drawn covered wagons designed for this terrain did not have nor need brakes. But now, navigating mountain regions and war rubble without brakes, gravity exacted it's heavy toll on the convoy and horses. It was a disaster the first time these roads were traveled. Now, in going home in the opposite direction it became yet another physical sacrifice for the few possession they had left. Josep, a refuge himself, located a cousin and her two children in the convoy. They were children themselves when they last saw each other before WWI, when the Banat was not yet split apart. Politically re-arranged borders kept them from visiting relatives between Yugoslavia and Romania. The group accepted Josep with open arms for his experience and ability to speak fluent German, Hungarian and Russian. This was a significant asset. He was immediately accepted as their leader.

The war was officially over, but some remaining British and American air squadrons now stationed on German and Austrian territory made it their pastime sport to buzz and shoot, with .50 caliber machine guns, objects on the ground. The convoys of covered wagons were their favorite targets. Unfortunately, casualties of this type are rarely mentioned and fail to enter history books. As they continued their journey, Josep was of great help in navigating and negotiating with the Russians over the rights-of-way at road blocks, rivers, and railroad crossings.

For Josep's relatives, the trip ended in Romania in their hometowns of Lenauheim (Tschadat), Grabatz, and locations nearby, but now the next heartbreaking chapter in their lives was about to start. Living in Romania, which was now a Communist country under the rule of the deranged dictator Ceaușescu, was more than eye opening. He first confiscated all the land and most of the homes owned by German speaking residents. A great number of the 250 year old beautiful towns had been leveled and replaced with primitive high-rise apartments for the farmers now forced to work on the state managed "kolkhozes" (farmers collectives). The dictator also sent several thousand women, along with men who returned from military service, as slave laborers to the swamps of the Danube River Delta region of Baragan. Ceaușescu wanted them to turn the swamp into farmland. Many died under horrific working conditions.

The returning Donauschwaben born in the Romanian Banat were recognized as citizens, but housing or sheltering refugees from Yugoslavia was punishable by law. This meant that Josep had to say goodbye to his relatives and the town where his father and grandparents were born. In this region the Rosenzweig heritage dated back 200 years.

3. Shocking News From Across the Border

Official communication between Communist Yugoslavia and Communist Romania was non-existent despite the fact that the German occupying forces in their respective countries were long gone by 1945. Under the new rulers, indescribable horrors were dictated and carried out on local born citizens whose heritage happened to be German and who had coexisted for over 250 years with their Slavic neighbors. People persecuted in Yugoslavia risked their lives by illegally crossing the borders to Romania or Hungary. They became the only eyewitness news conveyors. Tito's "partisans," outfitted with rifles and machine guns, were legally permitted to plunder, rob, and kill the innocent and defenseless homes and landowners throughout the regions of the Banat, Batschka, Baranja, Syrmia, and Slavonia.

Their families were ripped apart. Young women and men age 17 to 35 were deported to Russia and placed into slave labor camps. I was 17 at the time. Mothers who were taken had to leave their children behind, suffering the greatest hardships with only a hope and prayer for reunion in the future. The confused and crying childrens' fate and destinations remained undisclosed. Countless numbers of these children ended up in South Serbia and were given Slavic names. Children under age 4 would forget their real names and were never found again.

German speaking people from Yugoslavia, Romania, and Hungary were shipped by rail in cattle and boxcars in the winter of 1944 to Russia and housed in primitive slave labor camps. The purpose of the abduction was to work and clean up war debris under the most stressful and unsafe working conditions imaginable. Malnutrition, accidents, typhoid and homesickness claimed thousands of lives. They lost their homes, their beautiful towns, their sense of community and order. Everything was brutally broken up. Tito's trigger-happy partisans, many of them teenagers, were free to come and take anything their hearts desired. Documents, church and town records, photographs, or any indications of the 250 year German heritage in the region were collected and systematically destroyed by the authorities.

Shocking News From Across the Border

No losses or destruction were ever documented or recognized by any world bodies or war crime organizations — even to this day.

The most heartbreaking history from Yugoslavia befell the people who were sick or over 55 years of age. They were systematically rounded up, put on wagons, and taken to different locations with only the clothes they wore. There they were locked into makeshift concentration camps consisting of the now empty, smaller houses at the edges of villages. These had been enclosed with six foot tall barbed wire fencing. The secured entrances were monitored by armed guards 24 hours per day. Without food and water these people perished by the thousands. As proud, independent and self-sustaining farmers and craftsmen in the past, it is indescribable what their suffering and torture was like. Some grandparents were allowed to take their grandchildren along. Their destiny was the same, and they too were doomed. Able-bodied men were forced to dig huge pits in open fields next to these camps for the dead bodies to be dumped in — absent even the recording or recognition of their numbers, names, or identity. Countless numbers died daily from starvation, despair, and unsanitary conditions caused by typhoid which was widespread. Most bodies were stripped of good clothing before letting Mother Nature take over the transformation of innocent human lives into dust.

Who was next in line to have their lives changed into a living hell? Females age 35 to 55. Men of the same age returning from military duty in the German army were summarily executed. Countless numbers were forced to dig their own graves in fields where previously they grew their crops. Now the only working age German people left in town also had to live in the camps, behind barbed wire fences, in the empty, smaller houses at the edge of town. They too slept on floors and lived on starvation diets. The 250 year old tradition and pride of Donauschwaben farming practices came to an end like a derailed train. Kolkhozes were established. Now as prisoners, making a decision of how to work the land was forbidden. All animals were rounded up and organized differently. Job assignments were ordered by authorities without agriculture knowledge or training. The Panonien Lowlands as we knew them — so loved, treasured and tilled — were now a total disaster under the Yugoslavian Tito regime.

My mother was 38 years old when she was ordered to leave her home — house

SHOCKING NEWS FROM ACROSS THE BORDER

number 363. It had been built by my father's grandfather, Anton Hemmen, in 1908 as a civic and gathering center for the town of Pardan. My father inherited it when he married in 1926. My parents undertook some remodeling after they married, and it became our family home and farm house.

Having lost most of their possessions during the daily looting by the partisans, people tried to save some of their best clothing by wearing them in two and three layers. It was impossible to keep any personal property. Orders were given to all remaining Donauschwaben women in town to lock their homes and line up in the middle of the main street. There were no more 35 to 55 year old men present in Pardan. An armed patrol of young partisan officials inspected the lined-up women and ordered them to strip their clothes off in front of them. The next order was to hand over their house keys. This tragic event took place in Pardan on April 18, 1945. The good wardrobes were collected and exchanged for torn, dirty rags with which to cover their naked bodies. Suppressing all emotions for fear of being shot, this bone-chilling event performed on innocent, once proud and self-sufficient people was a silent cry to heaven, but no one cared for their broken hearts — Communism was the new order!

Several hundred German-speaking women with Yugoslavian citizenship were lined up in triple file and marched to the concentration camp at the edge of town. Serbians, Romanians, Hungarians, and Gypsies were allowed to walk free and to stay in their homes. Only the Donauschwaben women were now officially prisoners in their homeland, regardless of being born with Yugoslavian citizenship. Being placed into tight living quarters with no furnishings, only the floor to sleep on, and very poor sanitary conditions, the prisoners became resourceful and quickly formed bonds to help each other survive. Prayers, religious songs, and hope to somehow escape the claws of Tito — known as the "red dragon" — were strong in everyone's heart and mind. The camp perimeter was under strict surveillance and watched by round-the-clock armed militia.

The prisoners' daily work assignments were mainly farm and field related jobs. The kolkhoz system proved to be very dysfunctional and yielded low production which naturally resulted in cutbacks for all. The inmates' diets were especially poor, and it led many to eat raw potatoes, beets, corn, and squash straight from the soil. Smuggling something into camp for others was with great risk.

Not all Serbs became Communists. When they needed day-workers, whatever the task, prisoners were forced to stand-in as free labor. My mother was often called to work at Swetislav Momçilov's butcher shop. He used to be our next-door neighbor, was my father's age, and a good family friend. Now he was the only meat supplier for the town. Nani was blessed with courage and quickly learned the skills of a thief. She learned to snatch edibles from the butcher shop when Swetislav turned a blind eye. Hidden in her clothing Nani smuggled whatever she food she had snached to share among her hungry friends in the camp. Living under this communist rule brought people together, created safety nets, camaraderie, and was the only way to survive.

Often, for no apparent reason, prisoners were exchanged between the concentration camps in the region now renamed "Vojvodina." When 5 to 10 year old children showed up in the Pardan camp, Nani knew how desperately they needed milk for their survival. From the butcher shop she stole her way onto the property next-door and snuck around undetected to collect some empty wine bottles from the cellar. By asking for an assignment to milk the cows she used unwatched moments to fill some bottles for the camp. While trying to cork a bottle for safe hiding, she was unaware that warm cow's milk had explosive power when closed up before cooling, and she ended up with a badly cut hand. With the protection of Swetislav, who reported to the authority that she suffered an accident on his watch, she went unpunished. There are countless stories similar to Nani's, but not all of them ended well, but rather in severe punishment.

Another incident involved a young Roman Catholic priest by the name of Wendelin Gruber. He was given an affidavit and traveling permit by the partisans to visit the concentration camps for the limited purpose of praying with the sick and dying and to give them the their last rights. He took the punishable risk on himself and smuggled small children out of camps in his backpack or hidden in his cloak. He was very bold and trusted his life to the hands of God. Father Gruber wrote letters to some Croatian, Slovenian, and Romanian Catholic bishops in Yugoslavia. He requested help from authorities at the Vatican in Rome, but no help

SHOCKING NEWS FROM ACROSS THE BORDER

came. Nobody listened or cared to interfere with Tito's brutality and the killing of innocent Yugoslavian-born citizens of German heritage. Wendelin Gruber's sentence for getting caught was severe punishment in a cruel, maximum-security prison. One day, on the way to the bathroom, he stole a half-eaten sandwich from a rat. He was badly beaten by his guard. Father Gruber miraculously survived, and wrote a book titled: "In the Claws of the Red Dragon." All the cruelty he suffered robbed him of his health and he died at an early age.

In my own family, we suffered tragic losses of family members during and after WWII. Great-grandmother Anna Hemmen, age 92, starved to death in a Stefansfeld camp. Her daughter, Margaretha Rosenzweig (my father's mother), age 70, and her daughter, Magdalena Berger, age 50, died in Molidorf. They rest in mass graves. My cousin, Hans Gille, age 17, and imprisoned in Sankt Georgian, had to work barefoot on a kolkhoz harvesting sunflowers. When he cut his foot on a stump, without the possibility of cleaning or caring for his wound, he contracted blood poisoning. His mother, Anna Gille (my father's sister), risked her life to escape out of camp to beg a Hungarian family for help. They were in

A Donauschwabian Diary

previous years her field hands and friends. Under difficult circumstances, they obtained some tetanus vaccine which could have saved Hans' life. Disaster struck again when Anna returned to camp. The partisans confiscated the injection serum, and as punishment for leaving camp without authorized permission, she had to watch her only son die an agonizing and very painful death. At the same time, her two daughters, Magdalena, age 20, and Maria, age 18, spent time in Russia as slave laborers. Only a few months later Anna Gille learned that her husband Johann Gille was missing in action in Bosnia.

For the imprisoned Donauschwaben to survive, they were left with only one choice — escape — as their lives were in jeopardy either way. With all worldly goods stolen from them, most relatives killed and buried in mass graves without so much as even recognition of their names, the only hope left was to cross the border from Tito's Yugoslavia to Ceaușescu's Romania and beyond to find freedom. In this table-top flat land, the only secret passage was through corn and sunflower fields on dark nights. Some Hungarian, Serbian, and Romanian men took the opportunity to be guides or coyotes. For payment they took wedding rings, earrings, or whatever jewelry people had been able to hide until now from the partisans.

Nani was very brave, cunning, and took matters into her own hands. She knew the territory and field parcels by heart. She helped a group of five mothers with children safely across the border to Johannisfeld, in Romania. Her former next-door neighbor, Swetislav, and his son Zdravko, fortunately provided her indirect help. Through them she was able to send a letter to me in Russia. It was returned with a postmark and forwarding letter "for Nani via Ferna" in Thüringen, East Germany, with the news that I had been released from the slave labor camp at Krivoj Rog, Russia. Word also came informing her that her husband, Josep, was in Johannisfeld. Nani decided it was now her turn to escape, but first she sent a message to her parents, Johann and Magdalena Loch, both in their late 60s and imprisoned in Stefansfeld. She urged them to cut all ties to Pardan, their beloved birthplace and homeland and to never return. They had passionately created their customs and traditions in this Europe's most productive agricultural region. She was forever heartbroken over not being able to help them out of bondage.

At the same time Josep left Lenauheim. He learned of the news from the escapees that going home was out of the question. He faced the new reality that he would now be homeless and poor. Only the clothes he was wearing and the little wooden box tucked under his shirt were his worldly possessions. He still had his health and deep trust in God that carried him forward. The wish and hope in his heart to find his family encouraged his walk to Johannisfeld. He would now forever say goodbye to his beloved flat homeland under his feet and entending beyond the horizon. Approaching his destination, he recognized the fields in Romania that he used to call his own. Deep sadness overcame him while he reminisced about the time a mere five years prior that he ploughed and planted wheat and corn. This soil yielded very rich harvests. He was the perfect steward of his ancestral homeland he so deeply loved. This overpowering reality prevailed as the town came into view.

4. In Johannisfeld, 1946

Political terms and language are designed to make lies believable. How could the political icons of their day, Roosevelt, Churchill, and Stalin, the "world leaders," proclaim peace and equal rights, when with the stroke of a pen millions of innocent peoples lives were distroyed? Josep and Nani, now 44 and 39, were lucky to have remained healthy despite their experiences. Miraculously, Nani's epileptic seizures suffered from 1939 until 1944 ceased without medication. She reached the 6 km border crossing separating Pardan and Johannisfeld in Romania without an incident or assistance.

My parents' 3 year separation ended at the home of her uncle, Johann Bagi, aunt, and cousins Leni and Lissi, who were lucky to have kept a roof over their heads. The family and her husband of 20 years enthusiastically welcomed Nani. First she told about the horrible desperation and life-threatening conditions our Donauschwaben were suffering across the entire Pannonia-

Lowlands. She told of how Tito's partisans were legally allowed, frequently at gunpoint, to kidnap, rape, and rob people. As she spoke, she appeared very positive and self assured. She radiated a changed character that made it clear she no longer accepted the traditional rules of subordination of any type, whether as a wife, to a husband, or father. She now clarified that her marriage was a 50-50 deal and that Josep needed to face a critical decision for moving on and rebuilding a future together, pointing out that all that was left of their previous inheritance and wealth was now in the grain bag she carried on her back. It was the one and only one out of roughly 200 they once used on their farm for grain transportation.

From Josep's perspective, life had taken a drastic turn. His wife was now empowered and liberated. The war's action had changed him and altered everything he had known. Becoming a soldier meant taking and following orders. He was no longer directing his employees and field hands. Owning the largest estate in the region brought with it responsibilities. The livelihood of many families depended on his success. Upon the arrival of the partisans, Nani had to take over his role and respon-

In Johannisfeld, 1946

sibilities, in addition to being the mother of a teenage daughter and managing the household.

Escaping from behind barbed wire enclosures and fending for ones self does not spell freedom. It is just another step along the bumpy road of desire and hope for a better and more secure existence. For my parents, the moment of truth came as they were counting God's blessing for being alive and realizing the most important value was in bringing the family together and walking the path to freedom hand-in-hand. After Josep promised to give up his drinking habit, which in pastimes was a major issue for Nani, along with my letter from East Germany, reunification of the Rosenzweigs began.

Following their short breather, and much-appreciated help from the Bagi family, Josep and Nani's next destination was the more distant and larger town of Gross Sankt Nikolaus, where Nani had distant relatives from the Loch clan. Walking on, the couple found no sunlit squares — only the reminder of the ancestral soils they were leaving behind via country paths as they crossed western Romania. Their deep understanding of agriculture now became a new strength as

A Donauschwabian Diary

they smuggled themselves through cornfields and vineyards to freedom.

After every prayer came a dream with the memory of the past and hope for the future. Arriving in the mostly German town of Gross Sankt Nikolaus without an address, but German as a common spoken language, it was not difficult to find the Loch relatives. Nani's last visit had been as a small child before WWI and before the split of the Banat arranged by Winston Churchill. The couple had a friendly but short stopover. They received accommodation and exchanged news. They received advice to go to nearby Tribswetter and meet Dr. F. Roth who would hire them as field hands. This was indeed valuable information, as Dr. F. Roth was a kind and friendly man who asked Josef and Nani questions about their heritage. My father showed the Doctor their most treasured possession, my letter to my parents from Thüringen.

After reading the letter the doctor remarked to the poor couple, "You must have had a high standard of living in Pardan, enabling your daughter access to such good education. She writes German with perfect grammar, something most of us were deprived off during the Hungarian regime." Most of the wages earned as field hands for

In Johannisfeld, 1946

the Roth's were paid out in provisions and some Romanian Lei which could be used to pay for a river crossing.

The money earned at the Roth's also helped them pay a coyote to cross the border from Romania to Hungary. Maps did not exist. As refugees it was helpful to cross paths with others in the same predicament, to learn of safe passages, directions, or what to avoid. Many more stops were made on their journey. Also as refugees, begging for food and shelter often resulted in hostility and threatening language. Nani and Josep's walk north was difficult, but they were grateful when farmers let them sleep in barns with horses, cows, or sheep. One night, as in so many before, one of their creepy sleeping companions, a little mouse, ate a hole into their bag. Was it there to catch a ride or send them off with an autograph?

They pressed on. Speaking Hungarian helped, but they had no intention of staying in this country, as their next goal was Austria. Now another challenge arose. How to cross the Theiss (Tisa) and Marosch Rivers at the city of Hegeshalom. With no Hungarian money, Nani paid the ferry with her gold earrings and her wedding band.

5. **Austria In Sight**

Josep and Nani never gave up hope of finding a better tomorrow, despite rejection and scornfulness along the way by local people in Romania and Hungary. The negative attitude was not unexpected as the citizens were putting up with thousands of refugees walking aross their land and knocking on their doors. The Austrian border town, Bruck an der Leitha, came into sight, but other refugees had warned that the place was hostile and unfriendly. Some people chose a detour and crossed the border into Austria illegally. My parents were very tired and decided to cross legally. The border patrol ushered them to a building which was not only a place of registration but a jail. Their arrival without any identification was punishable by Austrian law by doing time in this jail. They underwent a lot of screening questions, got searched and placed in front of a grumpy judge. The judge gave them two options. First: deportation; second: get bailed out by an Austrian citizen. Josep tried to put a word in for himself by telling the judge of his military service for the Third Reich in the "Heimat-Schutz" (home protection) of the Upper-Austrian region. The judge angrily quoted, "We no longer have a relationship with Germany."

Josep then pleaded for time to call on a nephew, to whom he was a godfather. Thus it was arranged, by mail, to notify Josef Berger, now residing in Wiener Neustadt. Josep and Josef last saw each other in Modish, 10 km from Pardan, when the godson was about 17 years old. He was the son of my father's older sister. Brother and sister disagreed during a visit over the upbringing of the teenager. His overprotective mother excused her favorite son from doing physical work at his parent's village inn and grocery store because he had an appendectomy. My father's prediction was that this young man would one day become the black sheep of the family.

During the German occupation of Yugoslavia in 1940, Josef Berger found a way to leave home. He volunteered as an assistant organizer moving the Bessarabian Germans out of harm's way from the Russians, "Heim ins Reich" — to their ancestral homeland. There was a stop-over camp in Semlin, across the Sava River near Belgrade. It gave me the opportunity during my high school time in Belgrade to visit my cousin Josef once during his volunteer duty. We never met again. He moved on to Germany in search of independence and an easy way to make a living. As the German war machine demanded more and more support materiel, mainly ammunition, young Josef became employed as a department head at an ammunition factory in Wiener Neustadt, and was exempt from the military draft because he had married an Austrian girl. My family lost contact with him. But now, my father requested his help in hopes that he had compassion for his godfather's predicament.

Josef arrived at the jail with very bitter disappointment instead of help. His words were, "I am sorry, godfather, for not being able to help you. With the end of the war I lost my job. I am without savings and had not joined the communist party in Austria. I played cards and gambled, and now can not feed my wife and two sons." It shook my father in his boots. With a broken heart he controlled his anger and said: "Leave immediately, you are the lazy black sheep in the family. Don't ever come into my sight again for as long as I live." The only good news Josef provided was that he had met his aunt, Anna Gille, my father's second sister in Vienna. She stayed in contact with him, and had recently found her way to his place.

After two weeks in jail, the judge presented Josep and Nani a third option: He would provide written permission allowing them to travel through Austria for the singular purpose of finding their daughter in Germany. My letter from Thüringen served as proof and put them back on their way. The exact dates and time my parents spent in prison in Bruck an der Leitha were not recorded and are impossible for me to verify.

Bruck an der Leitha became well known for being a critical information exchange station for refugees. Living in tight quarters with so many others facing the same challenges and sharing the same aspiration of freedom and reunification with their families, the most frequently asked questions were: "Have you heard from so-and-so? Where are you from? Where are you going? Can we go with you? Do you have any money? How far in the land would we need to go to find a paying job? We will pay you back!" Surviving hardship and poverty proved time and again that trust and honesty builds lasting friendships. The same trust and honesty had existed 250 years prior among the Donauschwaben as they traveled South during the mass migration known as the "Schwabenzüge." The difference between than and now was that then the resettlement was a planned undertaking by the Habsburg dynasty with order and for a purpose. Now people reversed the trip, single file, in chaos, with hardship, and in constant danger.

Nani was optimistic, never giving up hope to find freedom and a better future. Josep's feelings were negative. He deeply grieved his loss of his homeland and everything in it. Now poor as a churchmouse, how could he ever again be a free farmer working his own land? He said to Nani, "How can you imagine independence when we don't even have pot or pan to cook our own food?" Walking the jail grounds one day, they stopped at a refuse dump, Nani looked it over and found a piece of sheet metal about a foot square. She gave it to him and said, "Make us a cookie sheet out of this."

He was astonished and for a moment speechless. After taking a deep breath he said: "I have no tools!"

She said, "Here are plenty of rocks. You can choose one as a hammer. The flat chunk of concrete can function as your work table." Josep took her advice, and putting his talent to use, hammered the four sides of the approximately eighth-inch-thick sheet metal into a useful, watertight pan. Nani was delighted with his creation. It would serve her well for cooking simple meals over campfires. I still treasure the cookie sheet today every time I use it.

6. Nani and Josep Travel to Vienna

How they got to their next destination, and how long it took them, has been forgotten. Nani's wishful thinking was that the good people of Vienna would treat them well. Firstly, because they spoke the same language and had a shared culture, religion, and a similar work ethic. Secondly, because of the relationship to the Austrians and the Hapsburg dynasty, which had resettled their ancestors to the Panonia Lowlands in the first place. This had granted them ownership deeds to the very land, which, after 250 years, had been transformed from swamp into the pre-war "bread basket of Europe." Equally important, and not to be overlooked, was Nani's father's Austro-Hungarian military service before and during WWI, as well as Josep's conscription as a soldier for the Third Reich.

Sadly, now all of these facts were of no merit. The current political realities had drastically altered the lifestyle of millions of innocent people. Josep and Nani received indentification papers as official "refugees without privileges." It allowed them to travel within the borders. They were only allowed to seek employment in agriculture, domestic, or sanitation jobs, or to work on construction sites. If the employer did not provide housing for them, each refugee and their dependents had to live in obsolete military barracks. Homelessness, living in the streets or forests, was forbidden. In the eyes of the citizens and locals these foreigners were the "Zuagrasten" — generously translated as "uninvited travelers." More succinctly, they were not wanted and were subject to continual insults and sarcasm.

My parents took their official first step into freedom in Jedlersdorf, a suburb of Vienna, working as field hands and domestic helpers. Their employer, Mr. Petz and his wife, owned some small farm parcels on the outskirts of town and held a few domestic animals on the property. For accommodation, they were allowed a small room on the premises with a bed and a small wash basin with running water for drinking and taking sponge baths. For personal relief they used a nearby outhouse. The pay was minimum wage plus three meals a day. Earning some money was a step forward and a peek into

Nani and Josep Travel to Vienna

the future, regardless of the fact that the cruelty of life had reversed their positions from being the employer to employee. They did not complain. Mr. and Mrs. Petz were friendly people. Mr. Petz had recently returned from a prisoner of war camp in Canada where he was treated, well considering the circumstances. He spoke admiringly of the million acre farming system that he had been exposed to while assigned to work there.

Nani and Josep were using the streetcars on their time off to travel into town. The stores were not yet well stocked, but they were able to buy postage stamps and writing paper to connect with relatives and friends. Their "grapevine networking" paid off a thousand fold. Anna Gille, my father's sister, had been given a job as helper at a nursery-cemetery landscaping business in Kagran near Vienna. There she met Sepp Achenbach, the second young man from our home town Pardan, who had incidentally dated her younger daughter, Marie, before the war. Their living quarters were an abandoned wooden barrack located on the field owned by the nursery and were within walking distance of their workplace.

Great news came to them from Marie. She had been released from a Russian slave labor camp and was now working for a farmer, without pay, in Saxony (then in East Germany). Sepp volunteered to bring her to Austria. It required illegal smuggling, a dangerous undertaking. I was informed in Thüringen of Sepp's plan with the invitation to come with them. In the meantime, as the news took its time to travel and connect, Leni Gille, Marie's older sister, earned the privilege to come from Russia and was united with her in Saxony.

    I wasted no time in my departure from the town of Ferna — a region of Eichsfeld. My plan was to travel by train, leaving Worbis, to Illmenau, known as the largest quarantine camp near Frankfurt an der Oder, where I had previously spent time. My purpose for the detour was to find my cousin, Nani Bockmüller, who had allegedly been released nine months earlier from Russia. Unfortunately and very sadly, I received the heart wrenching news of her death at age 21 shortly after she had been promised to go home. The second hard-hitting blow came when I realized I missed my connection with Sepp and the girls in Saxony. I met the cruel farmer who said, "Hah, how many more people was I supposed to house and feed? You missed the deadline. They left yesterday!" Without the farmer offering me a drink of water, a bite to eat, or shelter for the night, I turned around and went back to Thüringen. In Ferna the Kotzke Family gave me a place to stay, until I had another chance to escape to the West.

7. Nineteen and On My Own

No one was concerned for my safety, least of all myself. From my participation in the many smuggling expeditions, through my friendship with Erich Kotzke and his family, I had learned my routes through the forests and had found the secret hole in the barbed wire fence dividing Germany. I carried my worldly belongings in my primitive, wooden, 21" × 9" × 13" Russian box. I left the town of Ferna in Thüringen, East Germany on my own for the second time to sneak into West Germany. It was time to say thank you and a painful good bye for the second time to the Kotzke family who had so graciously given me shelter and protection. I was well prepared and knew how to avoid getting in trouble at railroad stations with the police who randomly checked the crowd for "illegal people." They deported people from the western stations regardless of their destination. My insurance was a fake telegram held in my pocket stating that my mother had died and my aunt requested my visit.

I left at daybreak, passed by the Russian watchtower unseen, crossed the border through the hole, undetected, kept going and caught a train from Gottingen to Nürnberg, arriving on foot at the Rottenhof farm late at night. There I had a very emotional reunion with my mother's sister, Leni, her husband, Peter, and their daughter, Susie Bockmüller. They were also refugees from Tito's Yugoslavia and now worked as field hands at the farm. The biggest surprise for me was to find my mother with them. We all had been separated for almost three years. We thanked the Lord to be alive and the tears of joy flowed like rivers. Seeing each other we filled the small room with an atmosphere of hope for the future. Everybody had expected to see Nani, the Bockmüllers older daughter, with me, just like it was when we were children and connected like sisters. Instead I was the messenger of bad news, informing them that she didn't make it out of Russia and had died on January 8, 1946 at age 21. She will always be missed as the stronger and the prettier of the two of us and will remain an irreplaceable family member. There was no time for grief and mourning, tears flowed, and our hearts were broken.

8. Next Stop, Austria

Our visit was short. For landlords to express sympathy was inappropriate when hiring helpers. Job assignments were rule number one and time was money. The Bockmüllers were reliable workers, and it was time for us to move on. My mother was given a few days leave by the Petz in Vienna. She had hired Sepp Achenbach, a young man from Pardan, to assist her in getting me illegally, but safely, across the border from West Germany to Austria. Sepp was trustworthy and experienced from his previous border crossings with the Gille sisters from Sachsen in East Germany to Austria. He would later marry Marie.

On our second day after leaving the farm, my mother, Sepp, and I were able to board a train from Nürnberg to Passau. Unfortunately, my mother got sick with profound bleeding. We found a hospital within walking distance and luckily got her admitted immediately. One friendly nurse who saw that we had no change of clothes took me to the basement, gave me a bucket of water and a place to wash my mother's badly soiled clothing. Outside I hung the laundry over a concrete wall to dry. Sepp and I had plenty of time to sit around in the garden telling the stories of our lives while hoping my mother would recover soon and be able to continue the trip with us. A lady from the hospital staff was kind and gave us something to eat. Late in the afternoon, good news came from the doctor. Mother was doing well, but they wanted to keep her overnight for observation.

The next question was where are Sepp and I going to stay and sleep that night? He had no military discharge papers from the German army. When the war was over and the system had collapsed, every man had to fend for himself. Without identification, we had no other chance of getting an indoor resting place except to walk to the railroad overpass and join other refugees sleeping under the bridge. Luck was on our side the next morning. Mother got released from the hospital without charge, wearing her clean clothes and happy to resume the trip back to Vienna.

Sepp's networking with the other refugee's under the railroad overpass helped us. He learned how to get to the town of Wegscheid, the nearest location to the

NEXT STOP, AUSTRIA

German-Austrian border, known as the back door. In a wooded area past the quaint little town, we met a middle-aged man waiting with his large pickup truck for passengers. Sepp bargained a price for the three of us to be taken to the outskirts of Vienna. More and more people came. They had the same goal, to be safely trucked to Austria. I don't know what he charged but I still remember being packed very tightly, standing room only, hanging on to each other for dear life on a flatbed truck. Luckily for my mother she was in the middle, sitting on my wooden suitcase. Sepp and I stood on the edge. He wore a hat. I had nothing to protect my head from the draft. The driver knew his way well and avoided all the checkpoints between the American and Russian demarcation zones. The scenic landscape changed from woodland to flatland and everything in between. But the ride remained very uncomfortable through the Mühlviertel. Vienna, not the city, but rather Jedlersdorf, a distant suburb, was the end of our trip. Mother, Sepp, and I thanked God and the driver for the safe arrival. Sepp took the streetcar to Kagran to be together with the Gille girls and their mother.

Mother and I walked to the Petz's residence, where my father was anxiously awaiting us. Seeing each other after three years of separation was like waking up from a dream. My changed appearance, and seeing me as a grown up, was very emotional for him. Hugs and tears assured reality. "Now we are a family again," was his happy exclamation. For a well deserved night's sleep, I shared the bed with my mother in their small room. Father slept in the barn. In the morning my parents introduced me to Mr. and Mrs. Petz. She politely informed me of my prearranged job, working as a "Mädchen für alles" (a maid for everything) at the Wegensteins' in Stammersdorf. Father's routine job did not change and mother was given an additional day off from her leave of absence to accompany me to my first "paying" job.

9. Stammersdorf, Austria

Mother accompanied me to the streetcar. She paid the fare in Schillings, as Deutschmark was now considered foreign money. The short ride and long walk along the Brunner Straße gave mother and me a chance to talk with each other in private. The Wegenstein estate was at the edge of town, where the owners greeted us excitedly. We were told my wage was to be paid monthly. I would receive three meals a day along with room and board. Depending on the season and necessary work in progress, I would get a Sunday off for visitation. Mother and I agreed. Politely they gave us some lunch, but I started feeling sick. My head was buzzing. I was loosing my hearing, and I felt a high fever coming on. My change of appearance caught everybody's attention. Mrs. Wegenstein was in her 60s. A very simple and kind person, she ordered their housekeeper, Miss Vera (about 50), to assist my mother in bringing me to the bed in my new room. The lady of the house personally called in the family doctor to come to my aid. He diagnosed an inner ear infection, one I presumably got from the drafty ride on the flatbed truck. He adminstered some medication and ordered a three day bed rest, which Mrs. Wegenstein promised to care for.

Miss Vera, a local neighbor, was the person who ran the household. Mr. Wegenstein was in his 60s, tall, sophisticated, stern and, compared to his diminitive wife, just the opposite of her. Mr. Fritz junior and his wife, in their early 30s, had a 7 year old son, Fritz. In winter they mainly resided in their restaurant-residence on the Lerchenfelder Strasse in Vienna. They spent more time in the suburb of Stammersdorf in spring, summer and fall at the time of the harvest, caring for their orchard and the large vineyards on the slope behind the estate. Well established large wine cellars had been dug into the mountain below the vineyards. The family grew and processed their own wine for the restaurant and for local sales.

It was fall and I started my day collecting a great variety of ripe fruit from the orchard. The best thing I could do for my health, while still recovering from malnutrition, was to eat my fill. During the day when Miss Vera did not need me in the kitchen washing dishes, peeling potatoes, or fetching something from the cellar, I was given various jobs to do in the cellars. On one occasion while I was kneeling on the floor in the basement selecting potatoes for dinner, I became aware of a person standing behind me. It was Mr. Fritz, speaking in a soft voice proclaiming his feelings for me. I jumped up like a vicious cat, looked him in the face and told him in a loud voice to get lost, or to collect the potatoes himself. I made no mention upstairs of the confrontation.

A lot of preparation was required for the upcoming grape harvest and wine making. Being involved daily, I learned a lot. Physically I became stronger and carried "Putten" (wooden buckets with shoulder straps) loaded with grapes down the slope along with the other hired help. I was familiar with professional wine making on a small scale, as my grandfather had made his own wine back home. I had loved following grandfather around and learning everything I could from him. Now I participated in winemaking on a much larger scale, and with a paying job. Pressing the grapes was done here with an electric-hydraulic tool.

To store and age the large quantities of wine, one needs many wine casks and barrels of different sizes. The Wegensteins had numerous ones with beautiful carvings, many of which I had to clean on the inside. They were impressive, tall, and constructed with something like a doggy-door in front. It could be removed for access to the inside. I crawled in with a burning candle in my hand, put it on the floor and was able to stand up straight. Now came the important job — to remove the crystallized deposits from the walls with hammer and chisel using both hands. For cleaning the outside I had to use a large, clumsy, very rough bristle handbrush. The wiping was done with a jute sack. Starting to work from the top down, I had to stand on a stepladder.

The lighting in the cellar was rather dim, and I didn't see or expect Mr. Fritz to come inspect my work. I only noticed his presence, when from behind his hand went up my leg. He miscalculated my advantage standing elevated on the ladder and that I had lightning fast reflexes. With my unmolested leg and all my strength I kicked him incredibly hard in the chest. He fell backwards and landed very hard on top of a stack of aging specialty wine bottles. I jumped off the ladder, walked past him and couldn't care less if he was hurt or how many bottles he broke in his hard landing. I went to the kitchen and surprised Mr. Fritz senior and Vera with my unexpected en-

STAMMERSDORF, AUSTRIA

trance. He turned around and in a commanding voice asked, "What are you doing here? Have you finished your assignment in the cellar?"

My answer in the same harshness came back to him: "You can ask your son that question!" Without waiting for another scolding I turned around, went to my room and closed the door behind me.

During the winter months I had more job assignments at the restaurant and at their city residence. I cleaned both senior's and junior's apartments which stretched across the second and third floors above the restaurant. In the restaurant kitchen, Miss Fani was the cook and ruling queen. Not even five feet tall, she let her presence be known. I had jobs helping her, like cleaning and chopping vegetables, peeling potatoes, and washing dishes. She was a good sport and was always friendly to me. Mrs. Wegenstein's role was to greet and socialize with her favorite customers. Thereafter she retreated to her little table and chair in the kitchen corner to relax with a bottle of wine. Occasionally she invited me for a talk and poured me a glass of wine for a toast. After getting to know her family well, it came as no surprise to me why she took to the bottle.

She was left out of any decision-making and responsibility.

My two year shovel training in Russia in the concentration camp turned into a sporting skill. I was happy to shovel snow in short sleeves and, to the surprise of the neighbors, with great speed. Little Fritzl giggled and laughed when I rolled him in the snow, and we made snowballs together. One day in summer, the doorbell rang at the lower half floor entrance. I was sent to check it out. The visitor came to see me — with a scream of joy I fell into the arms of my beloved maternal grandmother. This surprise I will never forget. She escaped from Tito's concentration camp in Stefansfeld in communist Yugoslavia. With a few friends in their early- and mid-60s, they walked through Romania and Hungary to Austria, hoping to find freedom and to be reunited with some of their relatives. The Wegensteins noticed that something important happened to me, and came to the kitchen, where I introduced my maternal Oma (as I called her) to them. Her appearance was shocking. All she had was the peasant clothing she wore and a scarf on her head. Her luggage was another headscarf tied into a bundle, which she carried on her arm, with only a few items in it.

STAMMERSDORF, AUSTRIA

The family left, and I took her to my room to give her something to drink and a bit to eat. My most heartaching question was, "Where is Ota?" — my grandfather, a man of great wisdom, and to me the best teacher and caregiver I had ever known. She was very much in control of her emotions and said without breaking down, "He died."

"Oma, how and when?"

In her story she told me that they had planed their escape during the time when the corn was approximately three to four feet tall to camouflage their movements. They had no water or food, and the captivity had taken its toll on their health. To survive, they ate the inner core of the still tender corn stalks. She was able to digest the fiber stalk, but Ota with his history of digestive problems got very sick. A patrol of Titos partisans found them stranded in their hideout and commanded them back. At the edge of town, in a small abandoned house with only some straw on the floor, they were allowed to stay. The patrol called it a privilege since Johann Loch was once the Mayor of Pardan during the time of German rule and was well known as a very wise and fair man to all nationalities. Oma was allowed to stay with Ota. No medical assistance was permitted, and he had to suffer an agonizing and painful death. She was then given a shovel and ordered to bury him herself. She laid his grave is in a nearby field. She marked it with a cross she made from two pieces of wood tied together with her shoelace. On it she wrote "Johann Loch 22. 05. 1879 – 30. 06. 1947" with a pencil she carried in her pocket. The patrol ushered her back to camp, from where she made her second life-threatening escape to find us.

I let Oma take a nap on my bed and went to the kitchen. As it also served as a den, I met Mr. Petz senior sitting in a chair. My begging plea with him was to let my grandmother stay with me. We would be happy to occupy the empty room on the street level with its separate entrance and work without pay. He got up, looked me in the eyes and said, "Thanks for asking – but the answer is no, your grandmother can not reside here." I thanked him and said that after she wakes up from her nap, I would take her to Jedlersdorf where my parents were.

Mr. and Mrs. Petz were not surprised by our visit, but rather that I wanted to quit my job so soon, after all it was their recommendation. It was obvious that we needed a

Stammersdorf, Austria

serious discussion about our next step in life. Mr. Petz suggested moving to the city of Vienna where building contractors were looking for people to work in the reconstruction process and clean up of the rubble left from the bombings. My mother was the first to agree to the plan. I seconded it with my "training" from my Russia experience. My father's question was about housing. Mr. Petz was well informed in refugee matters and shared that construction employees were living in school buildings. He had no bad feelings toward letting Josef and Anna move on to higher paying jobs.

Grandmother's willingness to sleep another night in the Petz's cow-barn was appreciated. In turn I planned on quitting my job and informing the Wegensteins the next morning when they assembled at breakfast time, informing them that my family had priority. Only Fritz's wife objected and asked me to stay on. She expected her baby soon and needed reliable service and help. She was a likable person, and I promised to find her a replacement. On the same day my father and I went to look for work and housing in the capital. My mother took her mother to one of the refuge barrack camps for registration and the receipt of an indentification with the assurance her stay was only temporary.

10. We Settle in Vienna

Upon our arrival in Vienna, Rella & Neffe, a construction company, employed father and me. This employment entitled us to housing. This was our first opportunity to gain independence and finally leave the aftermath of WWII behind us. Now reunited with my parents, we had new challenges. First, came the adjustment to our new living conditions. Housing for four families was in a single classroom of a prior elementary school. It lacked any privacy and had the wash- and restrooms in the hallway. Every person was given a military field bed, mattress, and one "Wehrmacht" (military) blanket. One picnic table and a bench served a three-person family. The young couple closest to the entrance received only a table and no bench. Our single male resident was given only a bed and the privilege to share the table with his neighbors. My parents and I had the choice area at the far end of the room with our very own window! The other three windows were shared, along with the three light bulbs hanging from the ceiling. The irony was that rent for these most primitive accommodations was deducted from my father's and my weekly earnings.

My mother had special talent in securing primitive furnishings for our new home. I have no idea how she obtained the small but sufficient cast iron cooking stove. Father managed to get the stove-pipe vented into an existing air duct higher up the wall. He and I collected wood from rubble and job sites. Mother's strongest desire was to cook food for her own family and to avoid soup kitchens. For utensils and household items, her favorite shopping was in Vienna's Second District on Tabor Strasse where the Jewish second hand stores were located. There she could bargain for deals and usually got a "Rabat" — meaning discount — because her last name was "Rosenzweig." She quickly found work as a domestic, cleaning a dentist's office. Soon she was recommended and hired to clean a jewelry store and workshop as her second job. Subsequently a lady with a small mailing business hired her for part time work packing merchandise.

Life in the city gradually improved. Restoration of the city's electrical systems made riding the streetcars once again reliable.

We Settle in Vienna

People depending on the gas supply were now able to cook and warm their homes. Austrians used stamps to shop for clothing. Refugees like ourselves were excluded from participating in this transitional economic system. The very popular "Caritas" and the "Lutheran World Organization" were our salvation. Their gifts were welcomed, practical, and much appreciated. However, the clothing we received rarely fit. So next came the alterations, requiring creativity, needlecraft skills, and extensive patience. All alterations and sewing had to be done by hand. Obviously, improved dress and attire afforded us access to more mainstream society and led to better employment opportunities and "acceptance" into the discriminating Viennese society. A German proverb says: "Kleider machen Leute," translating roughly to "clothes make the man."

11. Our New Address

Neumayer Gasse 25, 2A Ottakring, Vienna, Austria. We established many new friendships with people from many different Yugoslav cities, towns, and villages of the Banat, Batschka, Syrmia, Baranja, and Slavonia. We shared many stories. Most importantly, we learned from each other new ways and means of stepping into our new lives and dealing with daily challenges. Our shared common denominator was hard work without complaint and minimum wages.

We worked 8 hour, 5 day work weeks with cash payouts on Fridays. Father and I went by streetcar to the "Pop-Hof." Our identification cards were checked when crossing the demarcation zone. We were allowed free passage upon presenting our work permit, but traveling through the Russian Zone en route to our job site was always stressful. People with specialty skills or able to speak the Russian language were more likely to be kidnapped and deported. The job site was a very large apartment-complex damaged during bombing raids and now in urgent need of rebuilding.

The work was very hard. The site had been cleared of rubble. It was now ready for reconstruction. Father and I were assigned to deliver mortar and bricks in wheelbarrows to the bricklayers. The bricklayers were professionals and preferred to work in teams of two or three men. Company rules mandated a minimum daily work output. In order to earn beyond the minimum wages, the company encouraged extra efforts, called "Accord" work. This enabled the bricklayers to increase their pay. That was not the case for those of us supplying the mortar and bricks. My physical strength measured up, thanks to my improved diet of fresh fruit and vegetables I had received at the Wegenstein. The skills I acquired in Russia as a slave laborer also served me well. Nevertheless, it was a man's job and only a few women were working on the site. My father held a watchful eye over me, his twenty year old daughter. Father was average size, strong, and 46 years old.

12. Making New Friends

It was a pleasure to make so many new friends and to reconnect with old schoolmates by mail or in person who I knew from Pardan, Betschkerek, Werschetz, and Belgrade. One of my happiest moments was when I reconnected with Gisi (Gisela) Wiener in Vienna. I was one year older than Gisi, but at the German-Serbian Bürgerschule she was one year ahead of me. We shared three happy teenage years as residents at the "Raphael's Heim" in Belgrade. This was a very prestigious and revered boarding home run by wonderful German nuns. It provided a positive and cheerful setting for about twenty girls from different backgrounds and countries, focusing on the fineries of etiquette, manners, and writing.

Gisi, like me, was an only child of well-to-do parents. Her parents had owned a very successful textile trading business. At the beginning of the war, her father was drafted into the German army and one year later was killed in action. Mother and daughter not only lost their home, but also their business. They fortunately escaped to Vienna. Here Mrs. Wiener found employment as a cook at a fine boarding-home for girls. Gisi was hired as a helper and waitress and was happy to be able to stay with her mother. They had room and board and the occasional use of the house telephone. They worked 10-hour days and had one day per week off for themselves.

For us, each improvement in our living situation was greatly welcomed. Father helped some of those sharing the classroom, where we lived, put up some cheap, affordable room dividers. When it was time for our room to be divided and made more private, Mother and I were very happy. Father went out and bought some 2" × 2" lumber and corrugated cardboard. The hardest part of the project was carrying the building materials home on his back. A team of friends put up the wall and a matching door on one Sunday afternoon. The wall did not function as a sound-barrier, but its 6 foot height was a tremendous improvement in privacy. Our neighbors who were similar in age to my parents, the Weissmandls, couldn't contribute to the project but were thankful for the improvements. Vetter Peter, the father, was about 5' 4" tall,

Making New Friends

his wife, Bäsl Leni, about 5' 2", and their 22 year old son, Peter, a gentle giant who towered over all at 6' 2". They politely asked to put a few nails into the studs on their side of the wall for hanging clothes and towels. We in return walked through their domicile entering and leaving our room.

Mothers' shopping savvy continued to surprise us. This time she bought a second-hand sewing machine. It was an antique in good condition with accessories and full functionality. I was thrilled from the first moment I saw it standing on the table. Father's opinion was rather negative when it appeared, "What do you want to do with this old junk?"

Mothers reply was, "It will speed up the alteration work and help us with our needlecraft."

As time passed, Father warmed to the new family addition. Coming home from work especially late and tired one evening, Mother was greatly cheered, upon spying a father-daughter team at work. Father was hand cranking the machine, allowing me to do the sewing.

Our separation from grandmother took much longer than expected. The location of her housing, a former military camp, was not far away from vegetable fields. To earn a little money she joined a group of friends during the harvest. We decided to have her stay with us during the winter months, and we wanted her to benefit from the clothing donations. I missed her very much. However, company rules would not allow us to have an additional bed for her. Hence, I gave her my bed and slept on the bench or sometimes shared the bed with my mother. Oma, as I called her, was very helpful with all of our sewing projects. She also had infinite patience unraveling old knitted garments. With yarn thus salvaged, new sweaters were born. As soon as Spring arrived, Oma went back to work in the vegetable fields to earn a little income. From our city location she now met up with new friends and went to work by streetcar.

13. Trouble at Work

Our foreman ("Polier") at the Pop-Hof job site was a tall, husky, Austrian in his 30s who despised foreigners. He was also the construction elevator operator. The elevator was a primitive device. It consisted of a simple platform, without sidebars or walls, and was used to haul building materials up and down the outside of the structure. By no means would it have met OSHA standards. It was functional, and its usage bacame routine — a way of life. One day after the lunch break, I drove two empty wheelbarrows onto the platform, stood between them, pulled the rope, which rang a bell, which in turn alerted the elevator operator for a ride. To initiate a ride, a two inch steel bar in the middle of the platform was pulled out of its locking position. This maneuver disengaged the platform and turned control over to the operator. Imagine a theme park ride. This ride was even more uncontrolled than usual — a near free-fall from the 4th floor, with an uncontrolled hard landing. Upon impact the wheelbarrows flew left and the right. I had held on to the bar in the middle for dear life. Basically airborne, I landed solidly on my knee. Just by chance my father was on the ground filling wheelbarrows with mortar as I crashed down. It was a bone chilling moment for him. He confronted the elevator operator by yelling in his face, "Have you lost your mind? Do you want to kill my only child?"

For a moment silence filled the air. The man towered over my father, spit on the ground, laughed out loud, and said: "I can report you for failing to do your job. You have no rights in this country — no right to yell at a superior." I knew it was his revenge for turning down his overture for a date just the day before.

At home it was made clear that I should leave the job at once. Additionally, I had contracted an infection in both eyes from the dust in the air and the draft in the buildings. I had suffered from the same condition in Russia. Fortunately, in Russia, my condition resulted in my release to East Germany due to my unsuitability to work. I claimed "health reasons" for quitting my job, not the near-catastrophic accident.

Many of my girlfriends worked as domestics for families of high-ranking officers who were part of the occupying armed forces corps. I went to the Services Information Office and was promptly offered a position working for a French family in Ottakring, which was in walking distance from my home. The pay was less than at the construction site and only for 5 hours per day for 5 days per week. The family lived in a modern 3-bedroom apartment on the second floor. By 9:00 in the morning the family had departed. Madam was a teacher for French children. She took their three year old son with her. Madam spoke German fairly well. Her husband spoke none, and I was unable to communicate with him. Madam and her son came home for a one hour lunch break at midday. On her way home, she shopped for groceries to prepare a simple hot meal. After the boy had a half hour nap, they would depart. I had my lunch, finished cleaning, and as an extra bonus, I would take a bath. The job became habitual. I left before the family returned home. I locked up the apartment and left the key to the apartment manager, Mrs. Huber. She had become a friend. Mrs. Huber was in her 60s, a war widow, very friendly but in failing health. I would make her some tea or soup or run an errand at a local store for her. She was thankful for my help and friendship.

Months passed and I learned that my pay was less than what my girlfriends were making who worked for British or American officers. The school year ended and Madam gave me their upcoming schedule. She would leave for the summer to France with the boy. I could stay on, cleaning the apartment for her husband. On her return for the new school year, she would bring her second son with her. I requested an increase in pay. Her answer was no. I was told my pay depended on the rank of the officer, and my pay was determined by his unit. I agreed to stay on only until I found another position. My plan was to wait this situation out, and then, with the help of my girlfriends, land a house-cleaning job for another military unit.

I was happy to have more time to spend with my grandmother. For my health she encouraged me to enjoy the outdoors. Already bored with waiting, I told my French family that Friday would be my last day. On Friday, I took the key to Mrs. Huber and said good-by. She was sad to see me leave. We stood in the courtyard, when all at once a handsome young man in his early 20s joined us in our conversation. Mrs. Huber introduced him as her son Eddy. Presumably aware of his mother's friendship with me he

Trouble at Work

asked politely, "What are you going to do next?"

I answered, "I don't know."

He said, "They employ people where I work."

"Where is that" I asked without hesitation. I assumed he was a cobbler, having watched him from the second floor working on shoes, always with his back turned towards the courtyard. What must have crossed his mind now shocked me: she must be a refugee if she is doing domestic work. He corrected himself and said: "I am sorry for not being allowed to give you the address."

His mother pleaded: "Please forget the rule and give her the address. She has helped me very much. She deserves help in return."

With no one in earshot and my assurance I would not reveal my source, he gave me the address. "OK, for Mother's sake — I work at the toothbrush factory Karl Eder, Kienmayergasse 15, Ottakring." I shook Mrs. Huber's hands, thanked both mother and son for their generous information, happily going my way, hopeful of starting a new chapter I my life.

14. My Lucky Monday

On October 3, 1948, I walked into the office of Karl Eder Zahn- & Feinbürsten Fabrik (Tooth- & Specialty-Brush Factory). The secretary, a lady in her fifties, greeted me. The room was small, furnished with two well-organized desks, shelves on the back wall, and a counter from where she handed me an application to complete. She stood reading over my shoulder as I completed the form. In an angry loud voice, her face reddened with anger as she shouted at me, "How dare you attempt to apply for a job in a factory as a refugee!"

Simultaneously the door behind me opened and an elderly man in a business suit entered. It was none other then Mr. Karl Eder, the owner himself. Having overheard Miss Fanni's loud and ear-piercing rebuke, he swept her aside. He asked me directly where I was from. "From the Jugoslavian Banat" I answered. He was very friendly, and in a kind tone told me that he knew my homeland from back when he worked as a surveyor there, and met this pretty Romanian girl who became his wife 50 years ago. He went behind the counter to his desk telling Miss Fanni to type up a letter to the Department of Labor, stating in it that I was professionally trained and highly qualified to fill his factory position. He than signed the letter and turned it over to Mr. Ross, his 30 year old nephew, manager, and heir, who had just walked into the office. The two of us were sent to the Department of Labor in downtown Vienna for the required governmental signature. Upon our return, the legal document gave Miss Fanni the right to hire me with equal pay and no further fuss over my background. My fortitude and timing had produced a miracle.

I returned the next morning, met Mr. Eder in the office, and was introduced to Mr. Ulrich, the master mechanic and manager of the production floor. Mr. Eder introduced me as a descendent of an ethnic group renowned for their eagerness to learn, pride in hard work, and precise workmanship. From then on I reported to Mr. Ullrich. This was the first time I saw the inside of a factory. I had been given an opportunity to learn all the steps from start to finish for making fine tooth, hand, and clothes brushes. Mr. Eder periodically checked on my progress. It was always a pleasure to speak with him.

During my prior employment I had mastered the Viennese dialect. I spoke Viennese well and quickly blended in with the other 25 female and male employees. I was accepted as one of their own, and my background remained a secret. When Eddy and I met at work, we never let on that we had ever seen each other before. Mr. Ullrich couldn't care less where I was from. He was from Germany and not an Austrian. Unfortunately, six weeks to the day I was hired, Mr. Eder suffered a massive stroke. This silenced this kind and gentle man's voice forever. I never learned why he had granted me this extraordinary benevolence.

In stride with economic progress and the rebuilding of war-ravaged Austria, the Karl Eder Company qualified for help though the Marshall Plan. Through the Marshall Plan, modern machinery from the United States that was capable of producing plastic toothbrush handles was provided. This eliminated and replaced with automation the old cumbersome and time-consuming methods of cutting and processing toothbrush handles from sheets of celluloid. In early spring of 1949, the construction work for the building to house the new plastic injection machine began. This was sited in what had been Mrs. Eder's backyard, which once supported free roaming chickens and her flourishing vegetable garden.

With improvements on the horizon, workflow strategies and procedures changed from time to time, but the inconvenience was not too bad. My assignment was to do the finish polishing of the toothbrushes. It took a little navigating around a few corners to access the room, which in earlier years had served this very old building as a laundry room. It had a high ceiling and a single 12" × 18" window for ventilation, which faced the street. The room was narrow, with a large concrete stand in the middle of it upon which rested a polishing machine with two buffers. The machine was a belt driven contraption with the drive unit in the neighboring room. With pending vacation schedules and the pressure of completing the work, Mr. Ullrich assigned Mr. Neumann as my work partner for the day. Mr. Ullrich informed us that we would likely take our break earlier than usual as the electricians were expected to break a hole through the upper portion of the wall in our room to route the new electrical cables. When the time came to vacate the small room for demolition, someone was to inform

My Lucky Monday

us to stop work and close our station for a short while as the creation of the opening would create debris and dust.

With Mr. Neumann's help, the polishing went quickly, but after about three hours, Mr. Neumann became concerned about the knocking on the other side of the wall. He said, "I just hope they didn't forget that we are working on the this side." From his vintage point, he saw a crack opening and growing. I also became aware of the louder pounding, but ignored it, saying: "Nobody has come to warn us yet. We have no time to watch the wall cracking." As was customary, he always addressed me as Fräulein — Miss Rosenzweig. With only two more handfuls of brushes to finish, I focused on my work. I was sitting on a crate, the height of a bar stool, with only two inches between my right shoulder and the cracking wall. From Mr. Neumann's vantage point, he saw the rapidly growing danger approaching. Suddenly without having time to use a polite, formal phrase, he called out in horror: "Leni spring!" (Leni jump!). And just in the nick of time I did. A huge clump of bricks broke free and came down between my face and the buffing machine which was running at full speed. The bricks landed right in front of my toes between the spinning machine and me. The cloud of dust and debris, which followed, were a different story. It covered me from head to toe. Worst of all it made a near total mess of my almost-finished shipment of clean polished toothbrushes.

As luck and good fortune would have it, Mr. Neumann's alertness averted this close call. It left a hole big enough that the person hammering the wall and creating the opening became aware there were people on the other side. I loudly directed my frustration and anger loudly towards the ears of the assailant.

We shut the machine off. There was no damage to the buffers except the filth, dust, and debris. Mr. Neumann went upstairs to investigate the situation. I dusted myself off and went to the machine shop to let Mr. Ullrich know about the negligence of the electricians. Since I was not hurt, a more urgent task followed, namely to clean and re-polish nearly 1200 toothbrushes.

I entered the cutting room where the cleaning machine was located and to my surprise found two young electricians joking and flirting with the girls at their workstation. These electrician helpers were to have broken through the wall to create the opening. Goofing off from their job assignments was

My Lucky Monday

one thing, but when they learned about the hole their demeanor turned serious. They realized that their supervisor had arrived and done their work for them. The supervisor-electrician was arriving at the Karl Eder job site expecting to install a switch box. Not finding a hole in the wall to install it, he took on the hammer and chisel task himself. He had no way of knowing anyone was working on the other side of the wall or that creating the hole was to be announced.

The lunch hour passed, and I went back to the polishing room to clean up the mess. I piled up the bricks in the back yard, swept the mortar and dust as well as possible, and readied my station to polish the same order for the second time.

Later in the afternoon I heard someone entering to the room, a young man with an unbelievably beautiful baritone voice. He introduced himself as "Otto." He came to apologize for the incident earlier in the day. I stopped the machine to face him. There was no need for me to introduce myself, he had already heard from Mr. Neumann who I was. His voice mesmerized me so that I accepted his offer for a movie date to compensate for my troubles. It was the 7th of July, 1949.

15. Going My Own Way

I was happy with my job. The repetitious work offered plenty of time to think and plan a more fulfilling future. Dreams cannot stay on a wish list. Only activating them turns them into reality. Meeting Otto introduced me to a whole new world. I was ready to head fearlessly into my own new direction.

Work schedules before vacation time became hectic. I noticed Otto's brief presence at the Eder-project, but we had no time to talk. This situation left me with the big question of how and when were we going to meet again. Willy, one of the goof-off guys who skipped on the "hole in the wall" job, replaced Otto on a minor electrical installation. I met him during our lunch break. He apologized to me in a very strange way, believing the incident on his part turned into my opportunity to meet Otto. He further noted that his boss, Otto, had been assigned to another project for a while, but he could give him a message. At first I felt it was inappropriate to mix work with private matters, but I changed my mind and said I would write a note for Willy to deliver. All I had on hand was a piece of brown paper. In pencil I wrote the date that our vacation would start and when I would return, then thanked him for making his acquaintance. Willy's role was to mediate. The next day Willy was back smiling from ear to ear with a sealed note. In it, a brief note with a date, time, and the location on Mariahilfer Strasse and Neubau-Gürtl, inviting me to meet him for an evening city walk.

    My childhood dreams were actually being realized. I was now walking on those legendary old cobblestone streets of Vienna, the very same ones my grandfather had so fondly told me about as a child and that he himself had strolled as a young, proud Austrian cavalry soldier (Hussar) in about 1900.

16. Dating at Twenty-One

My girlfriend, Gisi, was more than surprised when I told her about the attractive young man I met at work under rather unusual circumstances, and who had invited me to a movie the upcoming Saturday evening. Otto and I were to meet at Mariahilfer Strasse and Neubau-Gürtel, a very busy intersection with a shopping center. Gisi wanted to have a glimpse of him. Her plan was to arrive with one streetcar and quickly transfer to another, disappearing in the crowd. Much later, when I introduced them to each other, Otto remembered her as the girl from the streetcar with the inquisitive, staring look.

On our first date to the movie theater, Otto was most polite. We addressed each other, as was customary, with the formal "you" ("Sie") and our first names. It was a lovely evening. After the show, he suggested our next meeting be a Sunday afternoon walk in the "Wienerwald" (the Vienna Woods) to catch some fresh air. I was overjoyed. Of course, I could only say "Yes".

At home I told my mother about the young Viennese man I had recently met at work, and his invitation for a walk in the Vienna Woods. She was not concerned, but rather happy and confident in my judgment of the young man. Mother and I shared a Tyrolian jacket and a trench coat. It was early fall and the weather was becoming unpredictable. I chose the trench coat to wear on my outdoor date.

For Otto this date was to test my love for nature and my comfort with the outdoors. Vienna's surroundings are beautiful, lush with vineyards, and many little old towns with tons of history. Fortunately, these were not affected by the war and its aftermath, and hence safe to visit. Otto offered me choices: Grinzing, Nussdorf, Sievering, or Neustift. It did not matter at all. All were entirely new to me. We took the streetcar to the end of the line. From there, trails and paths lead to delightful destinations. I was happy and overjoyed with the world. The light morning rain turned into a gorgeous blue sky with ornate clouds. For the first time since Thüringen, I walked beneath gigantic, towering trees. The tall grasses swayed in the breeze. Wildflowers in countless colors were everywhere. I delighted in every step. My guide narrated our journey to a little hut known as "S' Häusl am Roan." This destination that Otto had chosen transported me to a childhood "Hänsel und Gretel" fantasy world. We came across several puddles along the path. Otto gallantly offered his hand and helped me hop safely over them. When my coat got too warm, I took it off and he carried it for me. The hut was closed and not yet ready to serve snacks. Nonetheless it was a most perfect day.

    We returned to the streetcar just before dark. Sitting across from each other, absorbed in conversation, a golden sun set over the city. I was impressed to learn he was a glider pilot and an electrician trained and working for Siemens. We parted without setting another date, hoping to meet at work again.

17. Big Changes Ahead

Coming home from my first walk in the Vienna Woods I was so very happy. Instead of singing, I was more or less talking to myself, disregarding my father who was sitting on the bench by the table already a bit tipsy. I underestimated his vigilance when he asked, "Who were you with? It was not one of our boys!"

"No, he is Viennese," I replied. He mumbled under his breath and our conversation was over. Soon thereafter Mother and Oma came home from church.

For the next Sunday I was scheduled to stay home and host my Donauschwaben friends at our place. Like clockwork, friends from the Banat would gather — mostly to pass the afternoon and mainly to gossip. Most of them lived on the outskirts of Vienna and not near us. Without easy communications, it was hard to know who would show up. I expected my two cousins Leni and Marie. Marie's husband Sepp, Eva, Anni, and the two young men, Mats and Hans, who lived at the Speckbacher School within

A Donauschwabian Diary

walking distance of the Niemeyer School, were expected.

The weather was not bad, but only Matz and Hans came. Two is company, but as a trio, we decided to walk to the Mariahilfer Strasse to see a movie. Oma went to church, then met with her friends in our building. My parents took the streetcar to Schwechat to visit with my Father's cousin Franz and his wife Marie. Their daughter, Anni, chose to join them to see the movie playing in their area instead of seeing me and our gang. Everybody seemed to have had a good time regardless of the unpredictable Sunday gathering.

On Monday after work, my cousin Leni showed up at our door. She seemed distressed, unhappy. and angry. She was known for being domineering. When telling me I had been a bad hostess, my father interrupted her by asking why she had come to argue with us. She noted it was improper to have gone to the movies with Matz and Hans. Seeing my father's agitation, I tapped him on the shoulder and said, "Never mind, she is just jealous. For my part she can have both of them." I withdrew from the group.

18. Vacation Time

Gisi and I were happy to have a few days to ourselves to talk and to catch up with current events. I was looking forward to a repeat of the Sunday afternoon walk in the Vienna Woods that Otto had introduced me to. Halfway to the "S' Häusl am Roan" on this sunny day, she wanted to turn around, claiming she was tired of walking. She was not a happy wanderer, but with a lot of encouragement and prodding she proceeded. I did not reveal why I was so enthusiastic. The poor girl needed a rest day at home because she was so muscle sore before agreeing to another outing with me. I had loved to explore. I chose a little lake at the outskirts of the city for our picnic and this time with a much shorter walk. We spread out on a blanket underneath some majestic old oak trees. It was great to enjoy the beautiful landscape, relax, and to remember our carefree early teenage years in Belgrade at the private German Bürgerschule. Gisi and I reminisced and reflected on our innocent pranks and fun times. Then our conversation transitioned to dating, with Gisi raising the question as to why I was willing to trust a young man to take me on walks around the city and the Vienna Woods without knowing his last name.

Now that vacation had passed, my meetings with Otto resumed. He had promised me a walk through the First District at night. He pointed out the historic buildings, some dating back to the Roman Empire. He described the Roman ruins and the subsequent influence the Ottoman Turks had left on the city. I learned so much about the city's history. I was especially enchanted by his voice. He walked me home. This date was one more page out of my dream world. For our next Sunday afternoon date, Otto suggested a visit to one of Vienna's favorite city pools with its park-like landscaping. It had recently been restored and was now open to the public. This did sound appealing. I enjoyed Otto's company and the fact that I did not feel rushed into a closer relationship. My upcoming problem now was how to shop for a bathing suit.

First, I had to discuss the delicate subject with my mother. I did not seek my father's opinion, and he didn't ask about my dates. On my walk to work I remembered seeing a small window display in a simple store with a bathing suit for sale for a reasonable price and one for which ration stamps were not needed. I bought it without trying it on. At home I tried it on for my mother and Oma. The suit was clearly too short or my torso was too long. The suit was a pretty orange, knitted fabric, with two inch brown daisies. The back was two pieces separated at the waist. What made the suit too short was the "V" shape front connecting the top and bottom. Oma came up with a practical solution. Cut it apart. Eliminate the "V" and turn it into a two-piece bathing suit. To show your waist in public was unheard of in 1949 Vienna. Oma gave me some salvaged matching brown yarn from which I crocheted a finishing edge around the base of the bra and the top of the bottoms. Problem solved.

The weather was holding up, and it was still nice enough to be outdoors. Admission to the pool was free. Otto paid for a changing stall and used it first. I used it next. He had left his neatly folded street clothes on the bench. On top of his clothes were his wallet and identification. I peeked inside and read his last name and age. I was quite concerned about his reaction to my rather risqué outfit. The suit complemented my figure, showing off my very narrow 21-year-old waist. His very warm smile and the twinkle in his eyes noted approval of my attire. Our conversations were becoming ever more relaxed. It was time to transition from the formal "Sie" (you) to the informal "Du" (you). He told me his last name, address, and described his family. I kept it a secret that I has spied on his identification. He swam a few laps. The afternoon by the poolside was relaxing and went by all too fast. I didn't reveal that I could not swim.

    Suddenly a disturbance broke out. A group of five or six young men were after some young girls who were all already in the company of other men of their choosing. The trouble makers turned out to be Russian soldiers from a nearby base. Nobody wanted anything to do with them. When they approached us, Otto clearly protected me. Facing them I told them in Russian that it was against their own regulations to be there. I told them that I knew their commanding officer, and that I would report them and that for their own sake they should leave immediately. They departed promptly. I received a big ovation from the other bathers for putting them in their place and moving them along. It made Otto proud.

19. Surprises

One evening on the way home in early spring, Otto presented me with a small, lovely handbag made of black patent leather. It surprised me so much that I just said: "What is it for?"

His polite answer was: "An invitation to the theater." The Vienna Opera House and the Burgtheater, the high style icons of the music-world, still lay in ruins. Therefore smaller theaters and more commoner-oriented theaters, like the Volkstheater and the like, were in high demand. Seats at the Raimund Theater were sold out months in advance. So Otto had asked his mother to stand in line for him and get two tickets. This theater was in easy walking distance from their apartment.

When I told my mother about my next excursion and introduction to the Viennese way of life, her reaction was that I should have an appropriate dress. She liked the little theater handbag. She discussed the matter with her friend, a woman who custom-tailored clothing. The result was a navy blue dress with a bell-skirt, long sleeves and a white lace color, which flattered my girlish figure. Otto was pleased with the way I looked for the special evening. The operetta to be performed that evening was by Emmerich Kalman, a Hungarian composer who lived in Vienna around the turn of the century and wrote light classical music. His Csárdásfürstin (The Gypsy Princess) was much loved. Otto knew the Raimund Theater well. He told me of its history. Our seats were on the balcony with a perfect view of the stage. Marika Rökk, the Viennese-Hungarian leading lady, possessed the perfect charm and temperament as the gypsy princess. Her performance was a absolute crowd pleaser. It was such a fabulous experience for me — a lively performance, combined with such fabulous Viennese-Hungarian music. I enjoyed every minute. It was a spectacular evening. Otto also seemed to have enjoyed it.

During intermission when the lights went up, his mood slightly soured. Worried I asked: "Are you not feeling well?" He said: "No, just don't let anything spoil your happy evening." Even on the way home it was difficult for me to get an explanation on why his mood changed. Finally, he gave in and said: "Did you notice in the theater, two rows behind us, the lady eying us?" Not at all, with so many friendly and happy people all around us, my heart and soul had been swept away by the ambience and delight of the evening. "My mother spied on me. She bought three tickets instead of just two and spoiled my evening." At home Otto's father tried to reconcile the situation. The advice from father to son was to take his time to introduce the girl to us.

20. November

November is renowned for being Vienna's most miserable month of the year. The weather was foggy, drizzly, rainy, windy, and getting progressively colder. In Vienna this period is just known as "Allerheiligen-Wetter" (All Saints' weather). People dressed in dark clothing. They went to cemeteries to care for the graves of their loved ones, praying, remembering them with flowers, candles, or oil lamplights.

In my family, my mother kept a lit candle on the table with a few flowers in a vase to commemorate our relatives: grandfather Johann Loch, cousin Johann Gille, great-grandmother Anna Hemmen, grandmother Margaretha Rosenzweig, aunt Magdalena Berger, uncle Nikolaus Rosenzweig, uncle Matthias Loch, uncle Johann Gille, and cousin Anna Bockmüller. Their unmarked and unknown graves were in Yugoslavia and Russia. All of them were the victims of World War II and the brutality of the communists that had swept across the land. In years past, the graves in our cemeteries would have been decorated with beautiful wreaths of homegrown flowers. Now they were (and are) unattended and neglected, but not forgotten. Still our hearts and prayers were with all our loved ones who left their marks on Mother Earth.

My Oma announced it was time for her to move on. With the earnings she had saved doing fieldwork during the spring and summer growing season, she was going to buy a train ticket to West Germany. Her eldest daughter's family was employed as field hands on an estate. Their living conditions were less crammed than here in Vienna. She could contribute by caring for the animals. Also at her age, a little over 60, she felt she could still be useful. I was going to miss her very much.

Slowly, Otto introduced me to the varied and vibrant Viennese culture. Our favorite dates were visits to museums. Sometimes we went to movies or to the Urania, a public educational institute and observatory, which hosted lectures on the universe and related subjects. Much later he would admit I had won him over with my interest in astronomy. None of the girls before me shared this interest with him. The next step (quite literally) was to get to know each other on the dance floor. He was a member of a dance club and had been trained in ballroom dancing. It was a place to meet your friends and, of course, similar age girls. He bought me a membership and invited me to a dance. I wore yet another new custom made dress and looked forward to the evening. The baroque interior of the building was very impressive. Some of the music was American inspired and sounded modern. It required coordinated steps. We expected our start to be with something more familiar. Our moves were not converging. I had no formal dance training and from the first step on was not having fun. The evening was not very successful. Otto saw two of his friends only from a distance. They seemed not to approve of his choice of girlfriend. Not only was I wearing glasses, but that I was a refugee mattered too. On a separate occasion they confronted him directly: "Can't you do better than a 'Zuagraste'?" (translated from Viennese derogatively as uninvited/displaced person).

The situation did not discourage our friendship. During Advent, the four weeks before Christmas, cities and town all across Austria and southern Germany prepare for the upcoming Christmas holiday. They transform town squares large and small into beautifully decorated and festive

"Christkindlmärkte" (Christmas markets). Vendors raise tents and booths and decorate them with fir branches, lights, and ornaments. Merchants sell small items, usually handcrafted toys, candles, gingerbread cakes in many variations, and of course, Christmas decorations for trees and the home. Hot "Glühwein" (hot spiced wine) is sold everywhere. "Maronibrater" (chestnut roasters) are in full swing. These delicacies were sold by the half dozen in paper funnels made of newspaper. Their warmth not only warms the hands but also the heart and soul. The Christkindlmärkte are visited by all — young and old, shoppers and onlookers. In 1949 and 1950 the city of Vienna set up the Christkindlmärkt along the "Gürtel," a busy street far away from the usual site, the plaza of the Steffl (St. Stephen's Cathedral), as it was still badly damaged by Allied bomb strikes during the war.

The Gürtel was near Otto's home. Again, this adventure for me was something new. Our date was on the first Advent Sunday. We were onlookers, not big spenders. His mother handled all financial matters in his family. She decided how much out of his father's and his weekly pay contributed to living expenses and what was left was meted out as pocket money. Otto was kept on a short leash. He had two younger siblings, twins Brigitte and Horst, 15 years younger that he, whom he helped support and raise. His father spent much time away from home working in the Austrian provinces for Siemens Electric Co. at various steel mills, and was only rarely home.

The market did not flourish like in the years before the war. Nevertheless it offered a good holiday atmosphere. Otto and I strolled hand-in-hand among the crowd, delighting in our time together. We came upon a booth displaying hand made dolls and stuffed animals. Otto's attention was on the dolls. He wanted to buy one for his sister, but sadly was short on cash. My budget was tight too. It was not customary to barter, but then the salesman offered us a doll without clothing. The doll was made from "Kautschuk," a forerunner of plastic. Otto liked its smiling face and size. I urged him on to buy it. Now what? He looked helpless with his paper wrapped purchase. My answer was: "Entrust me with the doll, and I will turn her into a 'Rotkäppchen' (Little Red Riding Hood)." I had plenty of fabric scraps left from the alterations and sewing of my own clothes. "Just let me know when you want your sister's present ready." As we spent all afternoon walking around, he told me more about his family and their way of life. Among other peculiarities, his mother did not believe that a child, once school age, should have more than one toy, if any at all. In contrast, my mother showered me with dolls. I had a dozen in sizes from three inches to one and half feet tall in custom made dresses with porcelain heads and real hair. My doll house had been made by a professional cabinet maker. At age 14, I added the last doll to my collection. One similar in size to the one we just bought and also made of Kautshuk had been dressed as Little Red Riding Hood.

After "Allerheiligen" came the more cheerful St. Nikolaus Day, which was primarily celebrated on the eve of December 6. A gentle white bearded man dressed as a bishop would go door to door with his deformed, devilish looking helper known as Krampus. Parents would secretively invite the pair to pay a visit to their children. St. Nikolaus would ask if the children had been good. If so, they were rewarded with an apple, walnuts, or plums. If it turned out they had been bad, Krampus would strike their bottoms with his switches.

The Christmas Eve (December 24) tradition was to welcome "Christkindl" (Christ Child) into their homes. The family gathered behind closed doors singing carols and waiting for a bell to ring. Then the door opened revealing a surprise. A fir tree would have been decorated with lighted candles and colorful paper wrapped candies hung from its branches. Children hoped for toys, which Christkindl would have brought. Adults did not exchange gifts. For 7 year old Brigitte, the doll under the tree was an unimaginably great present. She was very happy. The doll was an unexpected surprise for the Wetzer family. The entire family until January 6, Epiphany, cherished the Christmas tree, the symbol of this great festivity. But as soon as the holiday was over, Otto's mother sat the doll on a shelf in the living room, announcing it was much better suited as a decoration, and too pretty to play with.

For my family my mother had bought three small pewter candleholders. Together they created a scene of St. Nikolaus in a sled bringing a Christmas tree. The little burning candles warmed our hearts and strengthened our hopes for a better future on our journey to freedom.

21. Awaiting Spring

Otto changed jobs, now working for a smaller company with fewer out-of-town assignments. He signed up for night classes at the "Technische Hochschule in Wien," pursuing his dream to become an "Electro-Technical-Engineer." He had started his training with Siemens Electric Co. before WWII erupted. For his family, this change was a financial setback.

Working in the countryside installing new electrical lines or maintaining electrical farm implements was often compensated, at least in part, with food products like eggs, a live chicken or rabbit, and sometimes "processed". One time his father came home from a weekend job with a live rabbit. For his 7-year-old siblings growing up in a bombed out city this was a most joyful occasion. They wanted to have it as a pet. This would not be possible in a single-room fourth floor apartment with a tiny kitchen, walk-in closet, and a multi-family shared toilet outside the apartment and down the hallway. On the second day, over the protest of the children, Otto took the bunny to his friend Poldi Gschladt's house who lived in another district of the city. Poldi's parents owned a small country style inn. To supplement their income during and after the war, they raised rabbits and chickens in cages in the courtyard of their property. These were valued food sources, and so was the Wetzer rabbit. It returned as fresh meat for a fine dinner on their plates. Brigitte insisted on visiting her white bunny. So the next time Otto visited his friend he took his little sister with him. In the courtyard of the Gschladt residence, she rushed from one cage to the next and saw no white rabbit. Extremely disappointed she began to cry. Mr. Gschladt senior took her in his arms and said: "The white bunny missed you so much, in his grief he turned gray."

Gisi and I attended evening classes at the "Privates Lehr-Institut für Berufspraxis" (Private Teaching Institute for Professionals) in the Argentinierstraße to gain some business bookkeeping skills. I was very successful, but gave up after one semester. My living conditions at home were too stressful to study for class. Gisi stayed on and soon landed a good accounting position. It was by coincidence that practically a year later I found myself again in the Argentinierstraße, now meeting Otto after his night class. I traveled by streetcar then waited by the main gate. His mode of transportation was his bicycle. He would walk me home, bicycle in tow. Time passed and he asked for the first kiss. He called me his "Lili Marlen."

22. Warmer Weather

I told Otto a lot about my homeland during that winter. Most of all, how you have to be born in a flat land to appreciate its beauty. The 360-degree horizon frames a picture of rich farmland all around you. Picturesque villages and towns six, eight, ten kilometers apart are like crown jewels. Horses were our most treasured animals. They provided great fun. In the winter they would pull large sleds loaded with family and friends across the snow-covered fields without consideration of speed or direction. In spring, when the agricultural work resumed, they would pull their heavy load. They went everywhere. They pulled wagons of all kinds. They responded to their names, as well as to commands, when ridden bareback. Their tall bodies were sleek and their legs slender. Their spirits were high — for galloping, slow trotting, or fast running.

I must have sounded like I was insulting the city horses. To me they were big, heavy, slow and only capable of pulling beer, milk and coal wagons. Otto recognized I was homesick. He suggested a visit to the racetrack on a warm sunny Sunday afternoon. I looked forward to this new adventure. We started out at the Mariahilfer Strasse and Gürtel. The streetcar was already packed. We chose to stand outside on the open platform. Passengers riding short distances or young riders like ourselves preferred to stay were the action was, rather to be squeezed like sardines inside the stuffy streetcar.

There was a large crowd at the racetrack in the Freudenau. Some folks were betting on the horses. Some were just onlookers like ourselves. When the horses were paraded, I picked my potential winner, and Otto choose a more attractive one. We picked our winners without betting money on them. My horse came in second and his last. It was exiting to watch the race and hear the people cheer. We had a good time and a perfect date. It was another fun afternoon.

The wonderful afternoon outing abruptly changed into a thunderstorm of harsh scolding by my father when I arrived home. He was angry because I had apparently ignored him on the streetcar. "Sorry father for not seeing you in the crowd", I apologized, "Where and when were you with me?"

Warmer Weather

"At the Ringstrasse standing behind you on the platform. You arrogantly did not introduce me to the young man you were facing and to whom you were talking." Otto had not met my father, so would not have recognized him. With my back to my father, I didn't realize he was standing behind me.

Having learned a lesson from the clashes with our elders, Otto and I knew it was time to introduce each other to our respective families, relatives, and friends. Otto picked a day when his father was home. Together we walked upstairs to the fourth floor in the 200-year-old apartment building where they lived: Kurzgasse 1, door 18. Mr. Rudolf Wetzer, Otto's father, warmly received me. He was familiar with my homeland, and knew our people from working in Neusatz (Yugoslavia) on a power plant installation for Siemens Electric Co. Otto's mother, Mrs. Margarethe Wetzer, was friendly too, but somewhat reserved. Brother Horst, at 8 years old, was curious. His twin sister, Brigitte, was shy and a bit skittish. I appreciated the invitation. After a two hour visit with Otto's family, Otto asked me out for a city walk and some window-shopping.

Earlier I had asked Otto for advice and assistance in buying a small radio. It would add a sense of home for our multi-family shared open-air room, and it would create an occasion to introduce him to my father and mother. I would be inviting Otto to our home to install the radio. The radio was to sit on a small shelf Mother had been given by the lady who employed her. Father had mounted the shelf to the wall on a space above our beds.

The meeting and introduction was to take place on a Sunday afternoon. Otto knew the School building from the outside. I waited for him by the entrance. The living conditions inside were shocking to him. My parents awaited us on the third floor. Mother greeted him first. Father got up from the chair by the window to shake his hand. Father saw in him a professional contractor. Otto knew he needed to make an illegal electrical connection between the lamp hanging from the ceiling to the wall and down to the radio. There was no outlet. The installation was completed and Father was the first to play music from the radio. Mother set the table with simple but inviting homemade cookies and coffee for the four of us.

23. Spirit of the Danube

One of Otto's best friends was Rudi Floder. They had known each other since kindergarten. Their mothers gossiped and soon everyone learned that Otto had been seeing a girl. Rudi's girlfriend was Fritzi (Federicke). Otto, Rudi, and Fritzi regularly met for social activities with their former schoolmates. Otto distanced himself from the group when he met me. Their relationship became somewhat strained as a result of my background and status — a "stateless" person living in Austria.

Nonetheless Rudi and Fritzi reached out and invited both of us to join them for a swim in one of Vienna's favorite Danube lagoons. The Sunday started out with brilliant sunshine. We arrived early in the afternoon at a picture perfect nature preserve. This locale was protected from improvements and commercialization. No wonder Viennese songwriters and city folk over the centuries loved the "Lobau" and other similar romantic places along the sometimes not so blue, but most famous Danube. The river is also known for countless historic sites and stories. Was Rudi's invitation meant as an icebreaker, a friendly initiation, or a spiritual Danube baptism?

After changing into our bathing attire, Rudi and Fritzi took us to surprise Hansi, Poldi, Erich and the rest of the gang. Otto introduced me to all of them and their girls. Poldi, the most suspicious one, warmed quickly about including a refugee into the group when he saw me in my two-piece bathing suit exposing my very slender waist. Fritzi and I quickly became best friends.

We had lots of fun at this lovely spot — in and out of the river as in the poetic Viennese muse: "drunt' in der Lobau, wenn ich das Platzerl nur wüsst..." Sadly, as a thunderstorm rolled in after two hours, our party came to an end. There was, however, enough time for the guys to plan the next outing and how to surprise the girls. It was called: "Eine Fahrt ins Blaue" (a ride into the blue).

Even with my improved wardrobe, Otto suggested that I should have an authentic "Dirndl," the traditional national dress. A dirndl consists of a jumper, blouse, and apron. Usually, printed fabrics and lively color combinations are selected for a dirndl. Winter styles are made of heavier cotton, often with linen, velvet, or wool, and usually with long sleeves. Summer dirndls have brighter colors, are made of lighter weight fabric, have short sleeves, and are more revealing. For me a dirndl was another step into assimilating into the Austrian society. Otto's former schoolmate Erich Skrabak's mother was a seamstress. She was a family friend who did some sewing but only on recommendation. Mrs. Skrabak was a warmhearted and friendly lady. She knew all about me before my visit. Otto and Erich knew each other from when they were 14 years old. They flew gliders together and used to build model airplanes on Mrs. Skrabak's kitchen table, in the process sometimes making a mess. Otto admired her generosity — Otto's mother would never have allowed such activities in her kitchen.

My mother was in favor of the dirndl. She liked it on me when I wore it on dates with Otto. The dirndl pleased Otto too. Our favorite dates were becoming all-day outdoor outings — hikes through nearby woods with excursions to castles and ruins on mountaintops. Such activities required some provisions. My mother would send us off with a large telephone book-sized aluminum box, "the Proviant-Dose". It was always filled with simple, but fine goodies. One of

A Donauschwabian Diary

Otto's favorites were the "Vanille-Kipfeln" (shortbread crescents). It was becoming increasingly fun to participate in outings with Otto's and my now many new friends. The outing destinations were trips by trains to the countryside or by boats on the Danube River to the "Wachau". Unfortunately, many of the historic places were still war damaged. Nonetheless, we had lots of surprises, fun, and pleasant memories to take home. We always looked forward to our next "Fahrt ins Blaue."

The following winter months were uneventful. We celebrated New Year's Eve with our group of friends at a cellar restaurant — good fun. But 1951 came with less pleasant surprises. February 9th would have been my parent's 25th wedding anniversary. Otto's parents were also married in 1926 on February 28th. Our parents had not met. Otto's parents suggested a date be chosen so that the parents could meet. Additionally, this would be an opportunity to celebrate both anniversaries. But most important to me was this should also be Otto's and my official wedding engagement. My father immediately rejected this suggestion and gracious invitation by Otto's parents. My parents had a double wedding with my father's sister, Leni, and he insisted he and my mother should be with the Bockmüllers. Besides, they had recently moved from Germany to Lower-Austria. "We owe them a visit!" he said. My father's rude disapproval shocked not only Otto and my mother, but also me. None of us had a hunch of his intentions. We were speechless.

24. Where To Next?

1951 was an uneasy time for the many innocent people in Europe whose lives had been so deeply and profoundly affected by WWII. Emotions ran deep. For Donauschwaben, moving out of refugee camps was of the highest priority. Decisions were being made to look for new beginnings elsewhere. Everyone hoped to create a better, brighter, and more fruitful future for their families. Promising opportunities came their way from far away places.

The German government worked out plans to resettle and integrate entitled homeless-stateless people. They proposed to provide low interest government loans for the construction of one- or two-family homes on government provided plots, each with a small garden. These land plots were properties cleared of war rubble and would later become the future suburbs of larger cities and towns. The authorities would decide building plans, layouts, and size of dwellings. Job opportunities included secured wages with built-in savings plans. To be eligible for this program, refugees were required to have already been residing in Germany or able to demonstrate legal immigration before a specific deadline.

France, Britain, and Australia opened their doors for immigrants under their own rules. Their criteria were primarily based on uniting friends and relatives by sponsorship. The USA and Canada used a similar sponsorship system. Obtaining permission to move to those countries required registration and assistance from religious organizations, which needed to provide in-country sponsors and a guarantee of a job.

Argentina and Brazil encouraged agricultural pioneers and settlers. Land was bought by a Swiss organization for them. Communities became well established but it took time, hard work, and a lot of trial and error to figure out how to make the land profitable. Today Donauschwaben are praised for their success and many have once again become happy landowners. They retained many of their traditions and German as their second language.

In Austria, our people who lived in larger cities took classes, learned various professions, prospered and demonstrated that they had invested their time wisely. Some of them sooner or later melted into Austrian society. Nonetheless the most depressing problem remained the chronic housing shortage. In cities there were waiting lists. These were based on prior citizenship or loyalty to newly established political parties. My father's two years of hard work in the construction industry did not qualify him to be in line for a home without an Austrian citizenship. It cost 6000 Schilling per person to acquire the Austrian citizenship to then be allowed entry to a waiting list for housing. There were three of us. It was out of the question to come up with such a sum.

The failed official engagement made no difference to Otto and me. We were devoted to each other. His father was proud of him. In a private father-son chat, he asked: "How serious are you about the girl?"

Otto's answer, "We like seeing each other. We have a lot in common. We share a love for the outdoors, but in order to be serious would mean improving our lifestyle."

His father put his right hand on his son's shoulder said: "If you take this girl, you will have a successful future." Otto took his father's advice to heart and lived by this principle all his life.

To discuss such serious matters, we decided on an outing to the enchanting forest of the Lainzer-Tiergarten. The weather in late summer was just perfect. We referred to each other as prince and princess, but to inherit our own kingdom meant waiting. Seated on our blanket, eating goodies from my mother's kitchen, we were suddenly surprised by an unexpected visitor. Within arm's length stood a majestic stag with enormous antlers as though they were a crown. His dark, friendly eyes looked down on us. We felt a peaceful and spiritual moment. I said to Otto: "He must be my grandfather's spirit, bringing us a message and blessing, just like the note I received from him on my way to Russia — 'never give up hope, it is the only way to come home.' We are at a crossroad to separate for a while. Lets hope it is going to be for only two years." The visitor vanished as quietly as he had come, leaving us with trust and hope. Our hearts were filled with love — this special moment was our private engagement without a ring. Our feelings for each other grew like swelling spring waters, reflecting our dreams for the future.

One day when Otto didn't show up for our prearranged rendezvous, I became concerned and walked to his home to see what had happen to him. His mother opened the door not looking very pleased to see me. She said, "Otto is in Mürzzuschlag. He was called to work on an emergency job. It is dangerous work at the steel mill. He told us about your intentions to move to America with your parents. My advise to you is to let go of him. It will no doubt upset him, in which case he could get distracted and have an accident at work. If any harm comes to him, I am blaming you for your selfishness." It felt like an ice cold shower had just been dumped on me.

My only answer was, "We feel that at 24 years of age we are fully capable of planning our own future." Wishing her a good day, I departed unaffected by her admonishment.

Otto knew my days off. I had made a reservation for one week at the small "Bärenwirt" bed and breakfast between the Semmering and Maria Schutz. A friendly family at the base of the Sonnwendstein owned it. The mountains all around were covered with lush forests and wild flowers, an ideal paradise for hikers. It took Otto only a 20-minute train ride from the other side of the famous Semmering to be with me for a carefree weekend. After telling him about my visit with his mother, he gave me his address in Mürzzuschlag.

Back in Vienna I was able to inform Otto, with my letters, about the progress we were making with our attempt to immigrate to America. There were many choices. One offer enticed me. It would have been to live in Utah as a companion for an elderly lady. Instead, my father chose a family in St. Louis, Missouri for me. They had three small children. His reasoning was that I would more quickly learn English. For himself and mother he decided on a wealthy couple in Fort Worth, Texas. He would be the groundskeeper and mother the housekeeper on their large estate. The couple spoke German. All sponsors guaranteed one-year room and board. The pay was not negotiable. My father, feeling like a pioneer, saw this as going that last stretch to freedom, and hoping that some of his friends and relatives would follow him. My Donauschwaben relatives and friends assumed my reason for going to America was to change partners, after being "dumped" by my Viennese boyfriend.

Moving means separation. It is difficult to say goodbye. I was sad to leave my job. My grandmother came from Brodersdorf in Lower-Austria to see us off. She watched us pack, tearless and quiet. It broke my heart to leave her behind. My mother's last shopping spree was three wristwatches and a camera. The remaining Schillings she gave to her mother.

It was the middle of September when we left Vienna for Salzburg with some fellow immigrants, now holding legal documents authorizing our crossing of two demarcation borders. Our destination was a closed military base. Under very well organized management, immigrants waited in turn to go in groups to the harbor in Bremerhaven to board military cargo ships for their voyage to America. We were informed that the waiting time might be as long as one week. I wrote Otto a letter with the news of the possibility of having a weekend together. He went home from work early to pack some clothing. His mother read his mind. "If you are going to Salzburg to meet that girl, you better not come home from there!"

Overnight visitors were not allowed in the camp. Otto suggested renting a room in a nearby private home if my mother consented. We spent two fantastic days exploring Salzburg together. At the "Imberg" overlooking the city, we stopped underneath a large crucifix promising to wait for each other. I said before we parted: "He carried the cross, now it is our turn for a while."

www.ingramcontent.com/pod-product-compliance
Lightning Source LLC
Chambersburg PA
CBHW071357160426
42811CB00111B/2204/J